Called to Be Stewards

Called to Be Stewards

Bringing New Life to Catholic Parishes

Patrick McNamara

THE LITURGICAL PRESS

Collegeville, Minnesota

www.litpress.org

<u>1   2   3   4   5   6   7   8   9</u>

Library of Congress Cataloging-in-Publication Data

McNamara, Patrick H.
    Called to be stewards : bringing new life to Catholic parishes / Patrick McNamara.
      p. cm.
    Includes bibliographical references and index.
    ISBN 0-8146-2889-3 (alk. paper)
      1. Catholic Church—Finance.   2. Christian giving—Catholic Church.
    3. Stewardship, Christian—Catholic Church.   I. Title.

BX1950 .M36 2003
253'.088'22—dc21

                                        2002035251

Dedicated to pastors everywhere

seeking new life

for those committed to their care

Contents

PART III
Advanced Stewardship

Acknowledgments

I write these acknowledgments on behalf of my husband Patrick, who, after a sudden and brief illness, died on November 16, 2001. He was hard at work on this book, updating and editing the pages when he passed away, leaving the overseeing of its completion to me.

This work on the growing stewardship movement in the Catholic Church was an important book for Pat to write. There was an urgency in his efforts to finish it and find a publisher, which he eventually did at The Liturgical Press, Collegeville, Minnesota. He begins his introduction to the work with the words "Catholics are in crisis," which indeed they are. He felt that the stewardship movement is from the Holy Spirit, who addresses this crisis by moving churches "toward dynamic and well-supported centers of worship, ministry, and spiritual growth to which Catholics of all ages are drawn" (p. xiv), a movement in which both clergy and laity become aware of a way of life that returns the gifts and talents received from God back to him through service to others.

Called to Be Stewards: Bringing New Life to Catholic Parishes was written with the help and encouragement of many enthusiastic supporters of stewardship. Pat had the privilege of traveling to many parishes throughout the country to interview pastors and their assistants, parish council members, and interested parishioners about their stewardship programs. All spoke frankly about their successes and difficulties in establishing and maintaining a viable stewardship program. He felt very indebted to them for their honest assessments, for without their frankness and forthright opinions this book would not be helpful to churches that want to begin a stewardship program.

Words of gratitude must also be extended to Matthew Paratore, director of the International Catholic Stewardship Council, who encouraged Pat to write this book. He gave my husband a list of churches that were already involved in stewardship at various levels. From this list Pat selected those for study and interviews. A special word of thanks also goes to the Lilly Endowment, Inc., which generously supported this work. In particular, gratitude must be given to Fred Hofheinz, program officer of religion at Lilly. He gave Pat encouragement and support for his study and the writing of this book.

Acknowledgment is gladly given to Mark Twomey at The Liturgical Press. As managing editor he extended many deadlines for the completion of this book. I missed them all except the last. He was at all times patient, hopeful, sympathetic, and very flexible at a time when I was discouraged by my task, emotionally distraught, and impatient about the completion of the book.

When I most needed her, Barbara Riley, writer and editor, came to my rescue when I could go no further. She made wonderful suggestions, polished the manuscript, and pulled it together for submission to the publisher. She was respectful of Pat's voice, his humor, and his passion for the stewardship movement. I cannot thank her enough for her expertise, sensitivity, confidence, and good humor.

Finally, I know that there are many others to whom Pat and I are indebted whose names I do not know but who would be mentioned here were he writing this. As he traveled to various dioceses, spoke at conventions about stewardship, and visited parishes, he was always welcomed with courtesy, full cooperation, encouragement, and interest in this book. *Called to Be Stewards: Bringing New Life to Catholic Parishes* is written largely because of these people, whose hard work, determination, generosity, and faith are examples for all those who want to embrace stewardship as part of parish life—making it a vocation, a way of life centered in Christ.

Following are the words of gratitude that Pat wrote acknowledging the help he received in writing this book.

Joan F. McNamara

I am most grateful to those who initially supported my proposal that resulted in this book. Fred L. Hofheinz, program director for the religion division of the Lilly Endowment, has been patiently encouraging from the start. Matthew Paratore, Secretary General of the International Catholic Stewardship Council, kindly lent his assistance in identifying the Catholic "stewardship parishes" that make up the case studies presented here. Special thanks go to the pastors of those parishes, who graciously agreed to my visits and the interviews that followed, introduced me to their staffs and parish organization officers, and facilitated my research in countless ways. My wife Joan, writing teacher supreme, caught many a grammatical lapse and was encouraging when I never thought I'd finish the book.

Patrick McNamara

Introduction

"Catholics are in crisis; the Church is in a state of peril and jeopardy; parishes are ailing; Catholics are bending the rules." All these are phrases sewn together from the titles of recent books and articles I have come across. Pessimistic exaggerations? Well, American Catholics *do* talk and behave differently than they did thirty years ago, and those shifts are captured vividly within parish life today. Ivan Shapiro, who spent virtually every day for a year at a New York parish, notes that Pope John Paul II, in his encyclical letter *Veritatis Splendor* (1993), "weighed in against those Catholic thinkers who stress individuals' freedom to make moral decisions based on their own consciences."[1] Page after page Shapiro takes readers through the lives of parishioners to confirm that "neither prelates nor scholars would have the final say on Catholics' freedom of conscience."[2] Pastoral consultant Father Thomas P. Sweetser, S.J., made this observation: "On most Sundays in most parishes, Catholics file into the pews with low expectations of being inspired, challenged, engaged, or motivated."[3]

Alongside these observations stands the priest shortage, well documented by Richard Schoenherr and Lawrence Young *(Full Pews and Empty Altars: Demographics of the Priest Shortage in United States Catholic Dioceses, 1993).* With the Catholic population growing by approximately 6 percent a year and the number of American priests available shrinking by 1 percent a year, the Catholic hierarchy works incessantly to encourage domestic vocations and seeks priests from abroad to serve in American parishes. In fact, during my visit to a Seattle-area parish, I learned that the Seattle Archdiocese is projected to drop to 75 priests in the year 2005 as opposed to 145 in 1996. Any parishioner these days is aware of how few priests are serving ever more crowded pews of worshipers,

[1] New York: Doubleday, 1996.
[2] Ibid.
[3] "Rx for Ailing Parishes: Change the Tone, Involve Everyone, Turn Outward," *Commonweal* (September 11, 1996) 20.

particularly in regions experiencing substantial immigration. No wonder Father Sweetser could later write about overworked pastors experiencing burnout.[4] Add to this that a pastor looking out on those pews knows how meager are the financial contributions Catholics make to their parish compared with those of their Protestant neighbors.[5]

Let me stop right here. I write this book as a bearer of *good news* about parishes today. The "stewardship parishes" you are about to meet stand as contrasting signs of a revitalization of parish life occurring across the United States, a development little documented in the face of "downside" reports like those above. In point of fact, parishes across the United States have found stewardship a way of moving toward dynamic and well-supported centers of worship, ministry, and spiritual growth to which Catholics of all ages are drawn. The parish case studies that follow illuminate *how* they have become so.

Since I write as a social scientist, I want to furnish a broader context for these case studies and explore ways of understanding the role of stewardship in American parishes. I first review pertinent findings of two bodies of research—one that focuses on religious congregations and their institutional contexts, and the other on attitudes and practices of Catholic laity as reflected in survey research. I then summarize accounts of what makes for vital, active parishes written by pastors, authors, and consultants with experience "in the trenches." Next comes the notion of stewardship itself, followed by two broad sociological portraits of American culture and society that will help us understand obstacles to implementing stewardship. I then introduce the case studies through a brief account of my involvement in this research.

Religious Congregations and Their Institutional Settings

A common way of classifying organizations is to ask why people belong to them. *Coercive* organizations, such as prisons and mental institutions, hold persons who are forced to be there. *Utilitarian* organizations provide members with tangible benefits, such as pay in a work-

---

[4] Thomas P. Sweetser, S.J., "The 'Good Enough' Pastor," *America* (September 25, 1999) 8–11.

[5] Dean R. Hoge, Michael J. Donahue, Patrick H. McNamara, and Charles E. Zech, *Money Matters: Personal Giving in American Churches* (Louisville: John Knox/Westminster Press, 1996). See also Patrick McNamara and Charles Zech, "Lagging Stewards," *America* (September 14, 1996) 9–14.

place or an education in high school or college. Churches exemplify
voluntary organizations: members gain personal satisfaction by fulfill-
ing personal goals (Girl Scouts, Rotary International) or by participating in something they think morally right (Amnesty International, Red
Cross Disaster Training). Nearly all voluntary organizations and their
leaders face the twin challenges of not only motivating members to remain active doing their share of organizational tasks but also, where
called for, encouraging them to be financially supportive.[6]

It is not surprising, then, that a growing body of research, much of it
ethnographic, focuses on how commitment is elicited from the members of a congregation. In a recent award-winning book, *Congregations
in Conflict: Cultural Models of Local Religious Life*, Penny Edgell Becker
analyzes twenty-three congregations in and around Oak Park, Illinois,
in the early 1990s.[7] "Who we are" and "how we do things here" as basic
issues yielded four "congregational models" with "core tasks" of religious reproduction, of community, and of witness. All four models
emphasized "religious reproduction," that is, provision of worship that
reflects a particular tradition as well as religious education. But when
members of congregations representing the first model, "House of
Worship," were asked what being a member of this church meant to
them and what role it played in their lives, 75 percent "immediately
gave a religious answer, most often saying that the church is, for them,
a place to worship and to express or explore their belief in God."[8]
"Most valued activities," they responded, "were religious education
programs or services held at Christmas or Easter."

As Becker points out, it is not that these church members reported no
sense of community or outreach ministries, but when asked what they
liked about their church, "nobody ever talked about outreach or com-
passionate ministry, just as they never gave any of the other reasons for
belonging that were common in other congregations."[9] One of the two
Catholic parishes in Becker's study fell into this congregational model.

The "Family model" elicited praise from members for a close sense
of belonging. "We are like a big family," was a common response. As in

---

[6] See Amitai Etzioni, *A Comparative Analysis of Complex Organizations* (Glencoe,
Ill.: Free Press, 1975).

[7] New York: Cambridge University Press, 1999. In 2000 this volume won the
Outstanding Book Award given by the Sociology of Religion section of the American
Sociological Association.

[8] Ibid., 57.

[9] Ibid.

the House of Worship model, religious witness was considered to be given mainly by the church's presence itself in the local community. In the "Community model," close relationships were also valued, but as a "community of values" the congregation's religious witness was expressed in policies and programs. "Leader churches" enjoyed a reputation within the denomination or among similar congregations for influence in developing policies and programs. Pastors in these churches were visible "players" in community affairs. Strong stands on issues such as institutionalized racism or AIDS outreach were characteristic of Leader churches.

Becker also allows for "mixed" churches, in which elements of two or more models are present. The other Catholic parish in her study fell into this category. What is significant, of course, is that motivations for participation and support by church members vary according to the type or model of congregation they belong to.

I cite Becker'research because it suggests a way of framing a core goal of the stewardship movement in the American Catholic Church. Becker's House of Worship model fits many a Catholic parish quite well. Given the central importance of the Mass and the sacraments in Catholicism and the historical emphasis on education, both through the Catholic school system and religious education classes for youth attending public schools, Catholic parishes have indeed been "houses of worship." Parishioners feel motivated by their need to worship God and to ensure that their children receive an education that includes knowledge of "the faith" and convictions about its practice. But under the impetus of the Second Vatican Council's Decree on the Apostolate of the Laity, together with the upward socioeconomic mobility of American Catholics since World War II, Catholic parishes can also be found within the parameters of Becker's remaining three models: Family, Community, and Leader.

As we shall see, adopting a stewardship approach can help "move" parishioners' motivations from a House of Worship mode toward a more widespread sense of "being a family" with obligations toward others. By encouraging participation, stewardship has the potential to help a parish express its values by growing in ministry outreach. Moreover, parishes that have practiced stewardship over a longer period, exemplified most clearly by the two "advanced stewardship" parishes (profiled in Chapters 6 and 7), move toward the role of a Leader-type congregation. In other words, a stewardship approach generates a dynamic, as the case studies demonstrate, that elicits a broader participation of members and a deeper sense of responsibility for the welfare of both the parish and the larger community as well. Becker also points out that "congregational models can be understood as different organizational forms that are compatible with and expressive of the individualism that has come to characterize much of American religion and that link this individualism to religious institutional repertoires for service, caring, and activism."[10]

As the next section will point out, American Catholics as portrayed in survey research certainly exhibit the individualism characteristic of Americans today. However, this need not be an impediment. A significant feature of stewardship is that it is linked frequently with (in some cases, sponsored by) "institutional repertoires" in the form of diocesan-generated support programs offering resources both to initiate and to advance parish stewardship, a phenomenon I discuss in Chapter 8. Far from stifling initiative, the American Catholic Church's institutional structure can be strikingly adaptive in helping parishes cut through individualistic attitudes of their parishioners. By adopting a stewardship approach, parishioners' participation appears to increase, with additional avenues of monetary support opening too.

Attitudes and Practices of Catholic Parishioners: A Sociological Portrait

Catholic parishioners are not easily persuaded to move to the higher levels of participation and financial support envisioned by stewardship. In a ten-year follow-up to their 1989 survey entitled "American Catholic Laity in a Changing Church," William D'Antonio, James Davidson, Dean Hoge, and Katherine Meyer[11] make a key distinction between the two-thirds of American Catholics who are registered in a parish and the one-third who are not. What difference does this make? A lot, it turns out. Fifty percent of registered parish members attend Mass at least weekly, as opposed to only 10 percent of those not registered. Fifty-three percent of parish members say that the Church is "one of the most important influences in their lives," as opposed to just 24 percent of non-parish members. Parish members by two-thirds say that they would never leave the Church, as opposed to the one-third of

---

[10] Ibid., 198.

[11] Meyer replaced Ruth Wallace, a coauthor of the 1989 study.

non-parish members. Parish members were much more likely to embrace the importance of the sacraments, devotion to Mary as Mother of God, the spirit of community among fellow Catholics, and a desire to have the younger generation grow up Catholic.

Unsurprisingly, parish members, while more committed to the institutional Church, still display the trend established since the mid-1970s of upholding personal autonomy and conscience in matters of individual morality. This trend is captured in the proportion of responses that agree with the opinion that *one can be a good Catholic* without following Church teachings on attending Mass, the use of birth control, abortion, marrying within the Church, donating to the Church, and helping the poor. It is also reflected in the percentage of respondents agreeing that *the individual has the final say* about divorce and remarriage, birth control, abortion, homosexual activity, and sex outside marriage. It is interesting to note that, while the percentages of those who hold those beliefs do not always reach 50 percent, they rarely go below 40 percent.[12]

Perhaps the least welcome news for Church leaders is that the percentages of those who hold that one can be a good Catholic without going to Mass or without obeying the teachings mentioned above have *risen* since 1987. James Davidson draws a sobering conclusion:

> For leaders who feel the church and its traditional teachings should be preserved, these findings represent a challenge to find new and more effective ways of interpreting the importance of the church. Until such means are found, indifference toward the church is likely to increase. For leaders who feel that the church and its current practices need to change, the challenge is to effect changes that will increase, not decrease, the importance of the church for future generations. Unless such changes are found, it is reasonable to assume that the significance of the church will continue to decline among lay people.[13]

Four researchers recently completed a national study based on parish records, focusing on young Catholics ages twenty to thirty-nine who

---

[12] William V. D'Antonio, "Parish Catholics: It Makes a Difference," *National Catholic Reporter* (October 29, 1999) 16.

[13] "Increasing Indifference to Church Is Concern," *National Catholic Reporter* (October 29, 1999) 15. See also James D. Davidson and others, *The Search for Common Ground: What Unites and Divides Catholic Americans*. Huntington, Ind.: Our Sunday Visitor Press, 1997.

had been confirmed during their adolescence. Ninety percent of those young adults continue to identify themselves as Catholic, and a majority are registered in a parish. Nearly one-third report attending Mass weekly. Impressively, 69 percent of non-Latinos in the survey and 66 percent of Latino young people say they attend Mass once a month or more. Around 60 percent report becoming inactive in church at some time in their lives. The authors say that "about half the people who went inactive [after confirmation] became active again before we interviewed them—48 percent of the non-Latinos and 45 percent of the Latinos."[14] Taking all twenty- to thirty-nine-year-old Catholics who became active in a church again (one half altogether), 86 percent of both Latinos and non-Latinos had returned to the Catholic Church, but the remaining 14 percent had switched to different Protestant denominations. All told, as the authors report, "about three-fifths dropped out and half of them returned later."[15] These recent survey portraits also indicate that despite the selective belief systems of many parishioners, most by far retain belief in such central truths as the divinity of Jesus Christ and the real presence in the Eucharist. In addition, a solid majority attend church at least once a month.

More worrisome than their beliefs, I think, is the declining importance of the Church to many Catholics. In fact, it is precisely this condition of Catholic parish life that underlines the desirability of renewal and revitalization. Renewal programs, however, must convince members that greater involvement in and support of their parish are both personally important and worthwhile, particularly in the light of research indicating that Catholic parishioners volunteer "only half as many hours per month as . . . Evangelical Protestants, and only about 60 percent as much as mainline Protestants."[16] New avenues of motivation are obviously required.

Practitioner Studies of Catholic Parishes

Father Patrick J. Brennan, president of the National Center for Evangelization and Parish Renewal, has written *Re-Imagining the Parish*

---

[14] Mary Johnson, Dean R. Hoge, William Dinges, and Juan L. Gonzales, Jr., "Young Adult Catholics: Conservative? Alienated? Suspicious?" *America* (March 27, 1999) 11.

[15] Ibid., 11.

[16] Charles E. Zech, Patrick H. McNamara, and Dean R. Hoge, "Lagging Stewards, Part Two: Catholics as Church Volunteers," *America* (February 8, 1997) 22.

and *Parishes that Excel* to portray churches that are not only outstanding but also serve as models for various aspects of parish ministry: participation in youth evangelization, multicultural and healing ministries, reaching out to the unchurched, parish governance, or a combination of these emphases. For Father Brennan, three "dominant images" are central to any transformative efforts on the parish level: "small communities, adulthood and adult faith, and family life."[17] He urges readers to stimulate their imaginations, to come up with "one *new* or *renewed dominant image* that will begin to influence your faith or your ministry."[18]

Father Brennan is a strong advocate of parishes working together with diocesan leaders to exchange ideas about what is effective in various areas of evangelization, gathering "regularly to swap ideas and models" around issues like these:

What are we doing for and with teens?

What are effective models for young adult ministry?

What is working in adult education?

What are some models of effective family-based religious education?

What are some models of reaching out to inactive Catholics?"[19]

Similarly, in *Transforming the Parish*, Fr. Thomas P. Sweetser, S.J., and coauthor Sr. Patricia M. Forster, O.S.F., "have been searching for paradigms that will bring new life to parishes," insisting that one way is simply not sufficient, and in fact "many options are needed that speak to different backgrounds, interests, locations, clienteles and situations."[20] Their ten imperatives for "moving parishes toward new life" include:

1. A survey of lay leaders and parishioners

2. Focusing information gathered so as to prioritize goals

3. Choosing short-range projects whose success will lift morale

---

[17] *Re-Imagining the Parish* (New York: Crossroad, 1990) 141.
[18] Ibid., 142 (emphasis in original).
[19] *Parishes That Excel* (New York: Crossroad, 1992) 117.
[20] *Transforming the Parish: Models for the Future* (Kansas City: Sheed and Ward, 1993) 212.

4. Confirming that the pastor is on the same page—working with staff, parish council, and key leaders

5. Exploring strategies to keep "creative juices flowing" with regard to programs and ministries

6. Developing sound organization to ensure that reasonable deadlines are set up with accountability for tasks finished on time

7. Strengthening a sense of ownership that encourages people to "share the load"

8. Encouraging social outreach or Christian service projects

9. "Tapping into the Spirit" to be alert to new directions and opportunities

10. Flexibility to be able to adjust to new circumstances and challenges.[21]

These authors are in demand as speakers and consultants. Their sound analyses and creative vision offer attractive paths of parish transformation that many churches have found immensely helpful. Similarly, I argue that stewardship, offered as both theological vision and motivational dynamic for congregational renewal, has spurred the distinctive revitalization experienced by the parishes featured in this volume.

The Notion of Stewardship

American bishops are no less aware of the need to revitalize Catholic parish life. Like the consultants cited above, they have endorsed creation of small faith communities within parishes under the banner of the RENEW program. Given the large size of many Catholic parishes, high priority has been given to such programs that foster interaction among parishioners in settings that deepen their understanding of Catholic beliefs and practices and encourage greater participation in the parish activities. However, individual bishops were also active in the early stages of what I shall refer to as the "stewardship movement" promoted by both clergy and laity who recognized stewardship ideals as a potent force for parish renewal.

[21] Ibid., 212–230.

From its founding by thirty-six diocesan development directors in 1962, the International (originally the National) Catholic Stewardship Council (hereafter ICSC) in Washington, D.C., under the leadership of Matthew R. Paratore, has steadily drawn more participants to its annual conference. In 1995 attendance reached one thousand participants. Each successive year has seen a 10 percent growth, resulting in over fourteen hundred pastors, development personnel, members of parish committees (pastoral, financial, stewardship, etc.), and many others participating in the 1999 conference in St. Paul-Minneapolis. Attendees listened to individual speakers and expert panels discussing topics such as "Introducing Stewardship in a Parish," "Stewardship for Families and Youth," "Discerning People's Gifts," "Building Relationships in Planned Giving," and "Preparing and Training Lay Witnesses," to name but a few. I was also inspired, at both conferences I attended, by the beautifully prepared concelebrated liturgy that closed the conferences, which helped to illuminate and seal the spiritual and communal context of stewardship for us all.

In 1991, ICSC began its first Institute for Stewardship and Development Summer Session. The Washington office also offers publications in both English and Spanish. The annual ICSC resource book contains high-quality essays on a variety of stewardship themes by experienced practitioners on both diocesan and parish levels. That many dioceses now have their own stewardship offices is often a direct offshoot begun with the encouragement of ICSC.

The stewardship movement, then, had been well under way when the American bishops published their pastoral letter in 1993 entitled "Stewardship: A Disciple's Response." Aware that the practice of stewardship was building momentum, they believed that it was time to craft a document setting out the *theology* of stewardship as a foundational statement that would affirm and further the *practice* of stewardship. In this pastoral letter they developed the basic New Testament image of the steward as "one to whom the owner of a household turns over responsibility for caring for the property, managing affairs, making resources yield as much as possible, and sharing the resources with others. The position involves trust and accountability."[22] To be a steward, as the title of the letter indicates, is part of the essential Christian vocation of discipleship begun at baptism. Each disciple is called to be a good steward of that vocation. What this means, say the bishops, is that

[22] Washington, D.C.: United States Catholic Conference, 1993, 20.

"each of us must discern, accept, and live out joyfully and generously the commitments, responsibilities, and roles to which God calls him or her."[23]

The bishops make it clear that living the life of the steward brings one to share doubly in the work of evangelization, helping to transmit the Catholic faith as well as engaging in works of justice and mercy toward those in need, while supporting the Church's institutions, organizations, and programs from one's own resources.

From this twofold sharing comes the familiar motto of stewardship: giving of one's *time, talent, and treasure.* Time and talent point to engagement in parish programs and ministries, as well as being alert for other forms of service and outreach—in other words, encouraging commitment-shy Catholics to volunteer their energies in community-oriented activities. The treasure aspect calls on disciples to provide financial support for the work and maintenance not only of one's parish but also of one's diocese as well as of the Church throughout the world.

This vision of stewardship is demanding and costly to practice. The bishops are quick to point to "the hostile values of a secularized society," which require stewardship commitment to run counter to "today's widespread consumerism and individualism."[24] That the bishops are proposing an overarching and challenging, indeed countercultural, theological vision is clear from this concluding passage of the pastoral letter:

> The life of a Christian steward models the life of Jesus. It is challenging and difficult, in many respects, yet intense joy comes to those who take the risk to live as Christian stewards. Women and men who seek to live as stewards learn that "all things work for good for those who love God." (Rom 8:28) . . . Central to our human and Christian vocations, as well as to the unique vocation each one of us receives from God, is that we be good stewards of the gifts we possess. God gives us this divine-human workshop, this world and Church of ours. The Spirit shows us the way. Stewardship is part of that journey.[25]

One reason for the bishops' resolute setting of stewardship in a theological context is to undercut any notion that stewardship is solely

[23] Ibid., 11.
[24] Ibid., 34.
[25] Ibid., 48.

about money. This association has, unfortunately, dimmed the appeal of stewardship even for some Protestant theologians and church consultants, as I have pointed out elsewhere.[26] Equally damaging is the custom in some Catholic parishes of trotting out the idea of stewardship only or mainly on Stewardship Sunday, when parishioners are admonished to be generous so that the parish can meet its budget. As I will emphasize throughout this book, *nothing damages the deeper theology and practice of stewardship more than associating it too narrowly with money.*

Each of the parishes profiled in this book has managed admirably to avoid this pitfall. Instead, they demonstrate how stewardship can serve as a guiding paradigm that shapes larger programmatic initiatives in each parish community. I believe the case studies in this volume will show that when a pastor wholeheartedly issues and sustains an invitation to actively implement this paradigm as a basic element of parish life, stewardship is capable of transforming a parish community along the basic dimensions of time, talent, and treasure, enhancing both revenues and numbers of parishioners volunteering. And yet . . .

American Society:
Why Is Stewardship Such a Challenge?

Every parish I visited struggled with stewardship. It was never easy to implement, and the process of becoming a stewardship parish was seldom a smooth transition. Resistance stood at every doorway, taking two primary forms. One concerned the time and talent dimension of stewardship, or how to move a parish beyond "the 80-20 principle," which means that a dedicated small number do almost all the work, moving from one position—now on the parish council, now on the finance committee, now as an usher or greeter or religious education teacher.

The second problem was persuading parishioners to be more generous financially. In *Money Matters* (see note 5), we documented what every bishop and pastor knew or suspected from their own experiences: When compared with members of other denominations in percapita giving to their church, Catholics are near the very bottom. Our 1993 national data showed Catholic annual giving per household giving

---

[26] Patrick H. McNamara, *More Than Money: Portraits of Transformative Stewardship* (Bethesda, Md.: The Alban Institute, 1999).

at $386 compared with $746 for Lutherans, $1,085 for Presbyterians, $1,154 for Southern Baptists, and $1,696 for Assembly of God members.[27]

In the course of studying stewardship, my discussions with pastors, staff, and lay members always came back to broader shifts in American society that formed daunting obstacles to stewardship implementation, namely, the two-wage-earner family, a rise in the cost of living (not least the increasingly bigger chunks of a family budget going to house and car payments and education), all adding to the pervasive busyness of people's lives. Fortunately, recent years have seen the publication of two major studies of American society that focus exactly on the areas challenged by stewardship and help us to understand why implementing stewardship is often such a struggle.

Robert Putnam:
The Shrinking of Social Capital

In his much discussed *Bowling Alone: The Collapse and Revival of American Community*, Robert Putnam amasses a staggering array of survey data to show that Americans, particularly in the 1990s, were reducing their "civic engagement." In a trenchant analysis that hit home to readers everywhere, Putnam observes:

> Organizational records suggest that for the first two-thirds of the twentieth century Americans' involvement in civic associations of all sorts rose steadily, except for the parenthesis of the Great Depression. In the last third of the century, by contrast, only mailing list membership has continued to expand . . . at the same time, active involvement in face-to-face organizations has plummeted. . . . the broad picture is one of declining membership in community organizations. . . . More important, active involvement in clubs and other voluntary associations has collapsed at an astonishing rate, more than halving most indexes of participation within barely a few decades.

He argues, quite convincingly, that the consequence of these trends is a diminution of "social capital," which he defines as:

---

[27] See Hoge and others, *Money Matters*, chap. 2: "Congregations and Laity: Profiles."

connections among individuals—social networks and the norms of reciprocity and trustworthiness that arise from them. In that sense social capital is closely related to what some have called "civic virtue." The difference is that "social capital" calls attention to the fact that civic virtue is more powerful when embedded in a dense net of reciprocal social relations. A society of many virtuous but isolated individuals is not necessarily rich in social capital.[28]

Putnam dedicates an entire chapter to religious participation, observing that "faith communities in which people worship together are arguably the single most important repository of social capital in America . . . nearly half of all associational memberships in America are church related . . . half of all volunteering occurs in a religious context."[29]

Yet, as impressive as churches may be as repositories of social capital, Putnam goes on to say that the historical trends in participation are declining. Evidence from the time [tracking] logs kept by Americans in 1965, 1975, 1985, and 1995 is telling. In terms of time spent on both worship and social activities related to religion, by 1999 we were spending only two-thirds as much time as we did in 1965.[30] Much of this decline can be attributed to the baby-boom generation, often analyzed by sociologists of religion. Putnam acutely observes:

> Active involvement in the life of the parish depends heavily on the degree to which a person is linked to the broader social context—having friends in the parish, in the neighborhood, at work, being part of a closely knit personal network . . . those supporting beams for religiously based social involvement have themselves been weakened in recent decades. The bottom line: While for many boomers privatized religion is a worthy expression of autonomous moral judgment, institutionalized religion is less central to their lives than it was to their parents' lives.[31]

Putnam goes on to show that the revitalization of evangelical religion has created a good deal of social capital in such congregations, though much of that capital is expended in their own religious communities rather than in the larger community.[32]

[28] Robert Putnam, *Bowling Alone: The Collapse and Revival of American Community* (New York: Simon and Schuster, 2000) 19.
[29] Ibid., 66.
[30] Ibid., 72.
[31] Ibid., 74.
[32] Ibid., 77.

In what is surely a surprise to many readers, Putnam reports that among both Catholics and mainline Protestants, church attendance is tied more to *secular* volunteering than to *religious* volunteering. Church attendance is associated mostly with leadership roles in secular groups. In other words, while the potential for social engagement is powerful in the churches, its actualization has diminished within the churches themselves.

In exploring the causes of these trends, Putnam points to several significant factors. For one thing, time and money limitations on two-career families have impacted individuals' willingness to participate in civic activities. In addition, twentieth-century demographic trends toward suburbanization and urban sprawl have resulted in long commuting distances for many families, making regular travel to sites of civic engagement increasingly inconvenient. Putnam argues that financial limitations, family time constraints, and urban sprawl account for about 10 percent of the decline in civic engagement and social capital. Another 25 percent, he believes, can be attributed to another twentieth-century development: Americans' fascination with, and absorption in, various forms of electronic media. (Interestingly, however, Putnam finds that decreased volunteerism is *not* prevalent among people who use the media for news and current events: those individuals are actually more likely to volunteer in civic life than people who use the media primarily as a source of entertainment.)

Most importantly, however, Putnam argues that nearly half the erosion in social capital can be attributed to generational change, a factor that other studies of religious life have emphasized, as discussed above. As he sees it, America's social capital began to erode during the postwar era, as the civically conscious and socially active World War II generation was replaced by "less involved children and grandchildren . . . a very powerful factor."[33] These social trends are interrelated, of course, as Putnam readily admits.

What can be done about these trends? How can we reestablish civic engagement and restore lost reservoirs of social capital? Any restoration will require "a major religious contribution," Putnam asserts, along with other major shifts. He echoes other observers of the American religious scene by pointing to the mega-churches. Although better known for bringing in thousands of worshipers weekly, their "leaders are very savvy social capitalists, organizing small group activities that

---

[33] Ibid., 283.

build personal networks and mix religion and socializing (even bowling teams!)."[34]

Putnam believes that another "Great Awakening" might help re-
vive religion's potential to spur civic engagement. More importantly, in
my view, he underscores the fact that the reemergence of social capital
within religious institutions can initiate social movements that in turn
regenerate social capital, as participants forge a strong sense of community identity and solidarity. Churches, then, are institutions that
have the potential to generate an enormous reservoir of social capital
and in doing so will produce energy for social change. As we shall see,
stewardship has many of the earmarks of Putnam's vision of a valuable
organizational social movement.

In addition, I think that Putnam has provided the best analysis for
understanding the time and talent challenge of stewardship churches.
Most Catholic pastors, in their increasingly busy lives, do understand
and appreciate how busy two-career families are. They know how far
some of their parishioners choose to drive on a Wednesday night to
attend an adult spirituality class or a parish council meeting after having fought traffic twice already in the same day. And pastors certainly
are aware of the influence of the ubiquitous television set, not to men-
tion the allure of the Internet. It requires a powerful motivating vision
to help parishioners see sufficient benefits for themselves, their families, their communities, both religious and secular, to volunteer for
ministries or to involve themselves in networks such as the Small Faith
Communities of the RENEW program.

My own view is that adoption of a stewardship approach provides
this motivating vision when it is properly implemented and pursued.
Just what this proper implementation entails will become clearer in the
case studies that follow. A further analysis focuses on the second major
challenge to stewardship implementation: resistance to parting with
our money! A splendid piece of research addresses just this topic.

Robert Wuthnow:
Money Is Such a Private Matter

Five years of research involving interviews lasting an hour or more
with over two thousand respondents went into the best analysis writ-

---

[34] Ibid., 411.

ten concerning attitudes toward the American Dream. In Wuthnow's study, people spoke candidly of their lives at work, how they took care of their finances, what it meant to be unemployed, what they learned from their parents, and what they hoped to teach their children. Wuthnow's *Poor Richard's Principle: Recovering the American Dream Through the Moral Dimension of Work, Business and Money* is the premier analysis of how people think about work and money and the pursuit of "the good life." Surrounding this pursuit is moral discourse about how we ought to live, that is, "personalized narratives, told to ourselves as much as to anyone else, to explain who we are, why we are good and decent human beings, and how we should respond to the choices we experience."[35]

Wuthnow begins a chapter entitled "(Not) Talking About Money" by alluding to taboos, once "guardian features of American life" but now "exposed and shattered." Examples of such taboos come readily to mind: prohibitions surrounding sexuality, legal barriers to interracial marriages or the struggle for a woman's right to participate in electoral politics.[36] During the 1960s many of these taboos broke down under the weight of massive social change. However, as anthropologists remind us, all societies have taboos. Sociologist Wuthnow asks the provocative question: In American society, which taboos remain in place? He expresses no doubt in his answer, "Money is perhaps the topic that remains most subject to deep norms of stricture and taboo. More than sex, health, death, or any aspect of personal life, it is the one most difficult for us to discuss in public."[37] We assume a strong sense of responsibility for our money, of course, but the taboo on discussing money means, "we receive little support from other people of the kind that might help us make better decisions or feel more confident about the decisions we do make."[38] Americans are aware that thinking about money "makes incessant demands on our personal time and energy. . . . A lack of money symbolizes constraint; the way to gain freedom is thus to have more."[39] Wuthnow's commentary is hard-hitting and provocative:

[35] Princeton: Princeton University Press, 1996.
[36] Ibid., 140.
[37] Ibid., 140–141.
[38] Ibid., 166.
[39] Ibid., 167.

> Handling money is just a grubby business, more detail to worry about in our personal lives. It makes no more sense to talk about it than it would to hold forth about brushing our teeth. But not verbalizing what we think about money also makes it possible to entertain private thoughts of a very different sort. We may have learned somewhere that money cannot buy happiness, but at a deeper level we believe it can. There is thus an internal contradiction in the way we think about money, one that leads us to want more and more, and yet to deny that this is what we really want at all.

The result is a heightened sense of pressure in our personal lives, "as if we are trying to break free of something we cannot fully identify."[40] Consumer rituals help us deal with this world of economic uncertainty. We believe that we can reduce unpredictability, which is a central feature of modern American life, by making "specific decisions about money . . . made largely on the basis of cues received from advertisers and marketing campaigns."[41]

If Wuthnow's analysis of our financial culture is correct—as I believe it is—then the upshot of the taboos and rituals surrounding money affect stewardship as a deep-seated resistance by parishioners of hearing talk about money from the pulpit. Every pastor knows that "he talks too much about money" is the one of the worst descriptions possible of a pastor and is to be avoided like the plague!

Because every pastor addresses men and women from the pulpit who experience the conflicting sentiments Wuthnow describes—these same people who seldom discuss finances, never mind money issues, with anyone—his "faithful flock" will only be made uncomfortable, if not resentful, by a sermon asking for money. Pastors have figured out that they can risk this sermon perhaps once a year, but not much oftener.

The Potential of Stewardship

Properly implemented stewardship programs can provide a way of dealing with and even overcoming some of the social and financial dilemmas described by Putnam and Wuthnow. I do not contend in

---

[40] Ibid., 168.
[41] Ibid., 188.

these pages that stewardship is somehow superior to other approaches to parish renewal that I have cited above, but rather that stewardship has a unique potential to support and strengthen other strategies. It does so by equipping pastor and staff with a foundational theology that encourages talking about responsible generosity with gifts of money and of time. Stewardship helps to open up what has been taboo, facilitates discussion in public settings, and encourages shared discourse with others about one's money and time and their uses—all in a context of gifts which have been given first to us and of which we are called upon to be responsible caretakers.

Stewardship thus becomes a powerful tool for helping parishioners think through what they have been doing, or not doing, with their financial resources, their time, and the talents (gifts) they have been given. "What is God asking of me (us)?" thus replaces "What is sensible here?" as a primary guide for fundamental decision-making. And in the process stewardship can become a very powerful remedy for what the surveys cited above have shown, namely, that for Catholics, religion seems less important in their lives than it was a few decades ago.

I was thus not surprised when my colleague and friend Charles E. Zech, in his recent book *Why Catholics Don't Give . . . And What Can Be Done About It,* gave stewardship top billing among the seven recommendations in his closing chapter: "The one best things the Church should do if it is serious about increasing giving among Catholics is to instill a sense of stewardship among its members."[42]

My Involvement: A Personal Note

My interest in stewardship dates from 1993 through 1996, when I was one of four researchers, supported by a grant from the Lilly Endowment, engaged in the largest study ever done of church giving in the United States. We gathered data from 625 churches, 125 each from the following five denominations: Assemblies of God, Southern Baptist, Evangelical Lutheran Church in America (ELCA), the Presbyterian Church (U.S.A.) and the Roman Catholic Church. When we finished gathering our data, each of us visited for several days individual churches that appeared to be outstanding for high financial support.

[42] Huntington, Ind.: Our Sunday Visitor Press, 2000, 132.

Among the churches I visited were several that had impressive stewardship programs, among them Father Tom McGread's parish, St. Francis of Assisi in Wichita, Kansas, which enjoys almost legendary status among Catholic stewardship advocates. (Because this parish is so well known and has been widely publicized, I have not included it here.) Some of these churches found their way into our book as case studies.[43]

I then discovered that no systematic study had ever focused on churches adopting a stewardship approach. The Lilly Endowment, Inc. kindly provided support for a further study I undertook in the fall of 1996 of both Catholic and Protestant churches that had adopted stewardship as guiding paradigm. Matthew Paratore, Secretary General of the International Stewardship Council in Washington, D.C., suggested four Catholic parishes to visit. I added others both in 1996 and in 1998–1999. My study of Protestant stewardship churches was published in 1999.[44] The present book is based on similar case-study techniques, involving visits of three or four days to a parish, carefully organized in advance. Each day was filled with tape-recorded interviews (beginning with the pastor), attending Mass and sitting in on meetings, and accumulating parish (and in some cases, diocesan) documents. All these became windows through which I tried to understand how stewardship worked in these vital churches.

Each parish, of course, was different. I have acknowledged these differences by presenting the case studies in three groups: (1) parishes that had most recently adopted stewardship (less than five years prior to my visit); (2) parishes whose programs had been in operation anywhere from six to ten years; (3) advanced stewardship parishes with a program in operation a decade or more.

I intend no evaluative hierarchy here; the two "advanced" parishes are not somehow better than those just beginning stewardship programs. Each has distinctive gifts as well as remaining challenges. The advanced parishes do illustrate somewhat more fully the transforming power of stewardship, both as illuminating vision and well thought-out ongoing programs. As will become obvious, these three categories of parishes are not airtight compartments. Some overlap exists from one to another: a "beginning" parish may rather quickly see a substantial increase in revenues and/or in volunteering (see Chapter 1). An

[43] See Hoge and others, *Money Matters*, especially Chapters 5 and 6.
[44] McNamara, *More Than Money*.

"advanced" parish may still be searching for ways to motivate a size-able minority of parishioners to give at all (see Chapter 7).

Each story reaffirms the understanding often shared by pastors experienced in stewardship: It is a slow process requiring diligent work to bear its promised fruit. All seven parishes underscore my conviction that if parish renewal is to grow within the American Catholic Church, stewardship is one of the most significant paths worth exploring.

PART I

Beginning Stewardship

Chapter 1

All of Us Have Gifts and
Are Called Upon to Use Them

CORPUS CHRISTI PARISH
FREMONT (HISTORIC NILES), CALIFORNIA

Tucked away in a quiet cul-de-sac two blocks off busy Mission Boulevard, Corpus Christi Church is nearly invisible. "Yes, we are a little hard to find," church members say. By contrast, everyone knows the location of Mission San Jose, the historic hub of an area that continues to draw visitors from everywhere. Corpus Christi Parish, which I describe from my visit in September 1999, was founded as a mission of the San Francisco Diocese in 1892 (in 1962 it became a parish in the new Oakland Diocese). It is located more precisely in the Niles District of greater Fremont, the fourth largest city in the San Francisco Bay Area with 200,000 residents. Its 94 square miles make it second only to San Francisco in size. Fremont is an easy drive from neighboring San Jose and draws many residents employed in Silicon Valley industries. The city takes pride in its rankings, among the nation's 100 largest cities, as first in home ownership and fifth in median home value. It ranked lowest of all 100 cities in households at or below the official poverty level. Fremont was recently named "The Most Kid-Friendly" city in northern California and the sixteenth best place in the United States to raise children.

The small community of Niles, according to the Chamber of Commerce's "Guide to Fremont," made history when the last of the tracks were laid connecting the Transcontinental Railroad from the Atlantic to the Pacific. Visitors can relive this event at the Niles Railroad Museum.

3

During World War I additional attention came to Niles when Essanay Studios selected it as the location to film their motion pictures. The most famous was The Tramp, whose star Niles remembers each June during Charlie Chaplin Days.

As one might expect, the Chamber of Commerce does not report very much about the Mexican laborers who came in the 1920s and early 1930s to work on the railroads or in the fields. Nick Jaramillo, seventy-seven, recalls the self-segregation of the larger ethnic groups in those days: "When they came to the Catholic Church, the Portuguese sat together. So did the Italians and so did the Mexicans who arrived a bit later." At Our Lady of Guadalupe Church, the Mexican men "did the whole Penitente thing, roping a man to the cross and acting out an entire Passion Play. My dad helped put on the pageant. Heck, he knew the lines of all the actors like Pontius Pilate and Herod, besides Jesus." When Nick returned from World War II, the Passion Play had moved to Corpus Christi Parish as the Mexican population expanded, "but they stopped doing it after a few years because they just ran out of room as the parish grew." He recalled fondly the services of the "mission band priests" who, in his youth, would bring the Mass from house to house to serve the area's migrant agricultural workers. "They were mostly Irish, but they had learned to speak Spanish pretty well."

The post-World War II years found many Latino parishioners rising in socioeconomic status. The G.I. Bill enabled veterans to acquire a college education unreachable before. By the time I visited in September 1999, Corpus Christi's 3,440 registered individuals were approximately 40 percent Latino, but that included several hundred recent immigrants whose primary language was Spanish. In fact, the entire Bay Area has seen a phenomenal influx of newcomers from all parts of the globe in the last ten years.

Stewardship Support from the Diocese of Oakland

The Oakland Diocese has risen admirably to the challenges posed by thousands of immigrant Catholics from Mexico, Southeast Asia, the Philippines, and Central and South America. Not only have new parishes arisen to serve them, but in 1991 Bishop John Cummins authorized creation of a Strategic Planning Group that brought together diocesan staff, pastors, and lay pastoral leaders from every parish. Three years of discussion and deliberation resulted in a booklet entitled *Strategic*

Challenges Facing the Diocese of Oakland and a statement of "Theological Presuppositions."

In a 1994 publication, "Faith in Service to the World: Recommendations for Action," three recommendations were made: (1) to encourage all Catholics, in discovering the meaning of their baptism, to accept "leadership in the church and elsewhere if called upon or chosen"; (2) to encourage a parish revitalization process (such as RENEW) in which parishioners "share with one another . . . pray together . . . and develop a sense of mission together [that] will be key to renewed communal and personal lives"; (3) "to place diocesan and parish energies and resources into establishing small participatory communities within our parishes."[1]

To help implement these recommendations, fifteen action-planning groups produced a long-term plan. Number one of fifteen initiatives recommended was to live as good stewards, designed to increase lay participation in both ministry and financial giving. Without this effort, "the diocese as well as the parishes will be unable to respond to pastoral needs." The following paragraph is a model statement of a practical theology of stewardship:

> Formation in theology of stewardship will encourage us to identify our gifts and contribute them where needed in service, ministry, and financial support. Wise and equitable allocation of both human and material resources within the church and society at large will become guiding personal and institutional concerns. Open and participatory decision-making will enable Catholics to assume financial and management responsibility for the church as good stewards, conscious of our accountability for the creative and dynamic life, which God has freely given to us.[2]

Recommendations for implementing these goals included establishing a diocesan stewardship function within the diocesan Office of Development "to encourage and help each parish to develop the spirituality of stewardship." A diocesan stewardship commission would advise and guide the carrying out of this recommendation. Stewardship spirituality "must filter down also into the small participatory groups within the parish described as root, eucharistic, and resourcing communities."[3]

[1] Diocese of Oakland, 1994, 4.
[2] Ibid., 5.
[3] Ibid., 6.

This overall initiative has borne fruit in recent years. Through the Office of Development under director Katherine King, together with stewardship coordinator Marge Perez, the Oakland Diocese has introduced a strong stewardship program. Reflecting California's ethnic diversity, all development and stewardship materials are translated into Spanish, and many into Vietnamese as well. Thanks also to the Strategic Planning Group initiative, the diocese is actively fostering the emergence of lay men and women previously underrepresented in the ranks of parish and diocesan leaders. In fact, stewardship at Corpus Christi owes its beginning to vigorous diocesan outreach and support.

Stewardship Comes to Corpus Christi

Father Timothy Stier, pastor since 1992, recalls hearing the term as the Oakland Diocese "began to talk up stewardship in the early 1990s":

In May 1994, all pastors in the diocese were asked to come to a workshop on stewardship. I remember thinking, one more program to worry about. And this one had a Protestant ring to it. I thought, well, we already have it, we just don't use that lingo. So I had an attitude going into the workshop. But I came away from it feeling much differently. It was really well done. Archbishop Thomas Murphy of Seattle, who helped write the bishops' letter on stewardship, spoke to us. So did people from our diocese, including lay people who were involved. I felt, yes, this was something worthwhile for our parish to do. Afterwards I called some people at the diocese and got information on how to start a committee. I had been focusing a lot on Small Faith Communities in our parish. I really pushed these my first two years here. I did so because, having been in charge of RCIA (Rite of Christian Initiation of Adults) in my early pastoral experience, I found that people would fall from Mass attendance, even leave the Church, without a support system. They needed a community to fall back on, which is where the Small Faith Communities come in. I gave a lot of attention to getting them going. This meant that I turned to active lay people in our parish to help take responsibility for getting stewardship started. The Garcias, Linda and Joe, had been involved with the Strategic Planning Committee of the diocese. They are very service-oriented, very generous. Linda served on our Pastoral Council at the time and was all jazzed up about stewardship. She called on her friend, Esther Martinez, who is good at organizing and follow-through, to help get the Stewardship Committee going. It finally got off the ground in 1997 and has been very active since.

The Garcias have been in the parish since 1971, drawn by "the welcoming and friendly atmosphere here. We never felt alone. Always a smile coming our way. The pastor at the time asked us to become active in the parish. Joe began by coaching Catholic Youth Organization teams." They recall the ethnic composition of the parish when they joined. "The Portuguese and Italians were here first. Some Mexican families, too. But the big increases in the Hispanic community came in the mid-1970s." A Spanish Mass was added around that time. The Garcias elaborated on their first experience with stewardship:

> Our involvement really picked up a lot when the Oakland Diocese invited us to take part in the strategic planning process. There we learned about stewardship, because that was the planning committee we chose to join. Several experienced pastors were members of this committee and shared what they knew with us, all the time, talent, and treasure elements. We found it a real struggle to assimilate it all. Our impression at the time was that some of the diocesan people overemphasized the treasure aspect, the dollars. Not enough emphasis, it seemed to us, on time and talent. Later, when we sent to the diocese our own parish proposal to implement stewardship, they sent it back telling us it did not put enough emphasis on treasure! What we were striving for, though, was a sense of ownership expressed in people taking charge of ministries, being on parish committees, and so on. Now we had also become involved in a Small Faith Community. In fact, delegates to the Strategic Planning Committee were chosen from these groups around the diocese. In our group we talked about taking ownership of giving and taking account of our resistance to giving more. But we knew that emphasizing giving would be hard. We even locked horns with the pastor of a much wealthier parish who told us it should be easy to stress the treasure aspect! Also, our pastor at the time—the one before Father Tim came—didn't understand stewardship that well. But then Bishop Cummins visited our parish, and when he was here he urged us to adopt a stewardship approach. Since then, as you know, we've been getting stewardship going. We have the ministry fair. And recently Father Tim has taken the lead by mentioning from the pulpit what his salary is and that he was taking on tithing, beginning at 5 percent. That made a

big impression on parishioners. They were surprised at how little he was paid and that he was tithing from that.

Several leaders I interviewed pointed to the key role of the Small Faith Communities that Father Tim had worked to establish. The theology of stewardship was a "natural" topic for discussion and helped members understand its significance for the parish. The previous pastor had asked Esther Martinez to represent the church on the Strategic Planning Committee because of her experience in another parish. Like the Garcias, she and her husband Joe were subsequently among the first members of Corpus Christi's new Stewardship Committee. Joe Martinez believes that the first crucial step to stewardship lies in a sense of ownership that comes from involvement, the notion that this parish is ours and we must take responsibility for its well being.

> I use the example of United Airlines and the labor problems they had a number of years ago. The airline was going bankrupt. But when the pilots were presented with the opportunity to buy stock in the airline rather than get a raise, they chose stock right away. Now the airline was theirs—true ownership. With involvement growing in this parish, people feel free under Father Tim to make suggestions and know they will be listened to. This is their parish.

The Stewardship Committee, the Martinezes pointed out, has helped encourage events that bring members of the parish together, whether it be donuts and coffee between Masses or a parish picnic. Such events provide a setting in which parishioners, mingling across ethnic lines, can get to know one another better. John Haley, one of the original members of the Stewardship Committee, remarked that encouraging parishioners to "share the load" assumed high priority. Paying off the parish debt, making repairs to the church, setting aside contingency reserves—all had to be pointed out in ways that had previously been soft-pedaled.

> We had to let the people know they had to do their fair share. I also suggested to Father Tim that his sermons be as concrete as possible. People may not be able to relate to tithing, but they know what it takes to keep up a household. And not everyone can contribute a lot—we have elderly on fixed incomes. They can only do so much. And Father took our suggestions. His sermons really improved.

Father Stier has been content to see lay leadership develop within both the Pastoral Council and the Stewardship Committee. He is especially appreciative of the liaisons between the committees that enable them to work and plan in the same direction. In fact, he admitted, only in 1999 did he attend his first Stewardship Committee meeting. Not only did he have confidence in the members and in their full disclosure to him of what the committee was doing, but "the problem has been that I literally do not have a free evening during the week. However, I've had to make time because we have had a kind of ongoing difference of opinion on the treasure issue."

Asking for Money: The Treasure Issue

Father Stier pointed out that the parish owed $130,000 to the diocese when he arrived. "There were times when the secretary could not pay the bills." By 1998 the debt was paid off, with the Stewardship Committee recommending to the pastor that the second collection, previously dedicated to debt retirement, be continued. A contingency fund for repairs and capital improvements thus emerged.

It was now time to address the issue of more stable parish financing, including pledging, which had not been stressed. Father Stier was planning to do so during the annual treasure campaign in November 1999. He said:

> We're at the point in our development of the parish where we need more money to operate the budget. I've only spoken of money twice in my seven years here. Both times it was to good effect. I've been waiting for the Stewardship Committee to come up with a kind of annual plan, but nothing has been forthcoming. So I've kind of been bugging them about it for the past six months. Two years I took the Stewardship Committee and some Pastoral Council members to a workshop by Father Joseph M. Champlin on sacrificial giving held in Pleasanton. . . . I was hoping that would really spark them. But I don't think they got it! My sense of their perception—and I told them this—was, if we just emphasize giving of time and talent, the money will follow. And they said, "Oh, no, that's not what we mean at all." And, true, it's not what *some* of them meant, but it *is* what some of the more vocal members meant, because I think they're uncomfortable hearing about money in church. And I understand completely just why. Some of

it goes back to years of abuse with pastors getting up—and I've worked with some of them—and all the time they talk about money. And every pastor my age or younger that I know, just because of that, is for the most part hesitant to talk about money very often. And some are not at all, which I think is irresponsible.

Lay leaders told me that, from their perspective, high priority was to be given to the concepts of ownership and empowerment. Those ideas needed to be disseminated to all parishioners as well as to the pastor. The recent past at Corpus Christi, prior to Father Stier's appointment in 1992, had been characterized by low parish morale, making ownership and empowerment imperative. As Joe Martinez put it, "So many people had become lethargic. We had to convince them that this was *their* parish." Only then would talk about treasure be likely to take effect.

Like many pastors getting started with stewardship, Father Stier found it a personal struggle, particularly where money was concerned:

> When I gave my big money talk two years ago, I wasn't asking just because the parish needed it, but because "You parishioners need to give it. When you do, it will change your lives. You know, if you really trust God enough to give five percent to the parish and five percent to the poor, your life will change." Now before I gave that talk, I'm not sure I believed that entirely. I was telling a pastor friend of mine about my misgivings of meeting our budget and he said, "Well, Tim, do you give to your parish?" I said, "No, why would I give to the parish? The parish pays my salary; I've given my life to this parish." He said, "No, you need to contribute five percent of your salary off the top to your parish every week and sign up for envelopes." I said, "Kevin, do you do that?" He nodded. So I had a little conversion. I'm not quite up to five percent but I'm close. And I told the parishioners I signed up for envelopes.

Giving: The Ethnic Factor

Father Stier was aware, of course, that many Latino parishioners were poor, particularly those who had recently arrived in the United States. Mild disagreement arose between the pastor and some members of the Latino parish leadership over how Mexican-American members should be approached. At issue were not just many families with low incomes but also the fact that giving "in the American way" was not a familiar practice among them. Opinions varied. Luis Cortez, seventy, a long-time parishioner, thought that Latino members "need to hear this is our home, our parish. They should understand the church, like their home, also has bills to pay, like utilities." Alfredo and Margarita Madrigal (she had been in the United States only a few years), while agreeing that financial needs of the church had to be laid out very directly, voiced a caution. Alfredo pointed out:

> So many just think the church is rich, and practices in Mexico are so different. People often give their pastor *los bienes* [goods], such as foodstuffs or animals—directly. Sometimes a parishioner will collect food and other materials from fellow parishioners to sell in the local market. Proceeds are then given to the priest. When they come up here, they find it hard to shift to direct money-giving for support of the church.

Financial stewardship has not been the only challenge facing parish leadership. Joe and Esther Martinez and Joe and Linda Garcia, along with others also bilingual and bicultural, see themselves as almost uniquely able to bridge any gap between Latino and Anglo parishioners. As Joe Martinez put it, "Some of the older Anglo parishioners, especially, wonder why we have a Spanish-language Mass at all. You know, the old 'Why can't they just learn English?' It really helps that Father Tim makes every effort to speak Spanish and offers a Mass in Spanish." Once again, bringing parishioners together through social events assumed considerable importance; a favorite is the now traditional coffee and donuts after Mass or a parish picnic. Heavily underlined, too, has been recruitment of Latino parishioners' "time and talent" into the ministerial life of the parish.

Time and Talent:
Stewardship as Involvement

In several interviews I heard very positive references to the first Ministry Fair, held in November 1998. Impetus for the event came from Bishop Cummins, who had declared the second Sunday in November as Stewardship Day "to celebrate the contributions of time, talent, and treasure by the faithful of the diocese." The Stewardship Committee met with representatives of each parish ministry to organize the event. They asked first that each ministry prepare a banner to carry into Mass during the initial procession. Each ministry or organization, in turn, asked its members for help in making the banner. "We had such a good time making that banner," a member of the Hospitality Group told me. "It really brought us together." Each ministry was asked to fill out an information sheet requesting its mission statement or objective(s), its vision statement, and its volunteer needs, along "with other information you feel would be useful." As an example, I offer the following from the information sheet of the Italian Catholic Federation:

> *Mission Statement.* We award scholarships to Catholic high school students to further their education, and grants to assist the developmentally disabled. We are a major supporter of Cooley's Anemia Research and Treatment Program at Children's Hospital in Oakland.

> *Vision Statement.* Family-oriented. Enjoy the fellowship of other Catholics by praying and playing together (we help the Bishop by contributing our prayers and money to further the education of young men in training for the priesthood).

> *Volunteer Needs.* We need new members as our membership has gone down due to the aging of our members. We encourage anyone to join. You don't have to be Italian, but have to be Catholic.

The Stewardship Committee also instructed each ministry to set up a table outside the church following each Mass to provide information and material for interested parishioners. For the first time at Corpus Christi, a parish directory, printed in both English and Spanish, was distributed at all Masses. It lists approximately thirty organizations, programs, and ministries, with a description submitted by each. Examples are LIFE Teen, with a Sunday Mass for youth at 6:00 P.M. followed by a LIFE Night gathering for high school students; Respect Life Ministry; St. Vincent de Paul, which, besides its familiar provision of clothing for the poor, serves lunches each weekday to the homeless just off the driveway entrance to the parish. As we have seen, key institutions at Corpus Christi are the Small Faith Communities emerging from the RENEW program "for growth in prayer and liturgical life, study, church ministry and fellowship." Together with the Movimiento Familiar Cristiano (Christian Family Movement), these communities have become vital instruments of spiritual formation for their members. As is the case in many parishes, Small Faith Communities have generated several new ministries as members reflect on how their beliefs should generate action. A Welcoming Committee sponsors the coffee and donuts after weekend Masses as well as the annual parish picnic. But it also explains the Small Faith Communities to new parishioners, encouraging them to visit a community meeting.

The Ministry Fair was apparently a huge success. One parishioner described the procession of banners as "electrifying." Many parishioners commented on the appearance of ministries they never knew existed and how the first-ever directory of ministries gave people a sense of how active the parish really was. As Father Stier observed, "You know, it was another demonstration of 'The Catholic Gift'—we're great at ritualizing things and it really makes an impact!" Many parishioners signed up. During my visit, plans were enthusiastically under way for a second fair.

Luzmarie Vallejo, president of the Pastoral Council, spoke of the challenge of encouraging Spanish-speaking parishioners to volunteer:

> Many who are newcomers are simply hesitant. They come from a different upbringing where volunteering is concerned. We know it's important to make sure that if there is a function, everyone should be invited, and that the event be bilingual if that seems needed. Those of us who are bilingual must help bridge our two communities. Spanish-speakers have to understand that the priest can't do everything, that they, and all of us, have to be active as well. What we all have to get away from is the notion that we're just consumers, attend Mass and that's it. The reality is that we're all responsible. People need help in seeing this.

A 2001 Update

As the fall of 2001 began, Father Stier was pleased that collections had risen a remarkable 50 percent since October 1998. A parish census completed in the fall of 2001 added a portrait: Approximately 850 registered families made up the parish. An ethnic breakdown showed 47 percent Latino families; 36 percent Caucasian; 12 percent Filipino; and 5 percent "other." About half of the parishioners in 2001 came from Fremont; another 25 percent claimed either Union City or Hayward as home; a remaining 5 percent cited Newark. Pledging continues as a crucial element of stewardship. Father Stier speaks in both English and

Spanish to set forth sacrificial giving as an ideal. These next remarks comprise an excellent model of a short stewardship sermon. The single focus is dedicated to the theme of sacrificial giving:

> When a few parishioners gather each week to count our collections, a fly on the wall often hears the counters exclaim, "Look at all the ones!" We receive around three hundred one-dollar bills a week, most given singly. For a few people, a one-dollar donation may constitute sacrificial giving, but for the vast majority it does not. So what *does* constitute it?
>
> 1. Sacrificial giving means giving back to the Lord a portion of our total income from salary, gifts, interest income, stocks and bonds.
> 2. "Sacrificial" means a donation that seems almost more than affordable; a donation that hurts a bit, a sacrifice.
> 3. Sacrificial giving uses envelopes provided by the parish as gift wrapping for our sacrificial gift.
> 4. Sacrificial giving involves planning the amount we donate based on the biblical tithe, meaning ten percent of our income as a faith-filled way to show our gratitude to God.
>
>   What I ask you to do this week is to consider becoming a *sacrificial giver* (if you are not already). To help you decide what to give each week, please pick up the brochure in the pew entitled "Planning Guide and Commitment Card." On the bottom left find your household's income. Let's say you earn twenty-thousand a year like me. Then move to the right to see what you are presently giving away. If I gave one dollar a week, that would be one quarter of one percent of my income. For me to become a sacrificial giver, I would need to give nineteen dollars to the poor and needy through second collections, charities, and the Bishop's Appeal. I ask each family this week to think and pray and talk about this, make a decision, and fill out the commitment card, tear it off and place it in the basket over the weekend.
>
> 5. As our Lord Jesus Christ shares his body and blood eucharistically, we, as members of his Mystical Body and as a grateful community, give back a "sacrificial" portion of what we have earned.

Both the Martinez and Garcia families were asked to take leadership roles in establishing a Stewardship Committee. Inspiration was sought from a call to discipleship beginning with parish leadership, but what *kind* of leadership was a critical issue.

Thus continued discussion of ownership and empowerment among parish leaders led in an important direction: treasure was to receive *less* emphasis than time and talent together. Stewardship, a bishop's letter emphasized, was not to be confused with sheer fund-raising. Once again, existent ministries and services were to receive emphasis. What turned out to be important was motivating parishioners in a context of stewardship properly understood, that is, not just financial generosity motivating everything else.

Father Stier made his own understanding of stewardship centrally important. He introduced parishioner Ronnie Duricheck-Amy, who shared her own story with the congregation. Like Father Stier's homily, her remarks are to the point; they convey an authenticity that inevitably commands attention and stirs reflection:

> As I prepared for today, I was struck by the recurring theme of "stewardship" as it relates to our families, our parish, and our community. In sharing with our parish community, and with my Small Faith Community, my time, experience, strength, hopes, talents, and yes, treasures, I came to realize that these are all vital parts of my faith journey today. . . . God has been very good to me throughout the years. I have never been without a job or a place to live, and obviously I haven't missed too many meals! This doesn't mean that life has always been easy. Far from it. Yet somehow through everything I have always known that God is taking care of me. It somehow only seems right that I have a responsibility to return what has been too freely given to me. In the past, when I would make out my check for the church, I didn't give very much thought to how much I should be giving. Then, a few years ago, Father Tim gave a talk very similar to what you have just heard, and he gave us a simple formula for calculating how much to give. I figured it wouldn't hurt to give it a try. Guess what? I wasn't giving what I should have. As I prayed about this, I realized that everything I have today is a gift from my loving God. Then the answer was simple. Today I still use that same formula to figure out my contributions. I have also come to treasure the time that I am able to give to various parish activities. I cannot begin to imagine my life today without my Small Faith Community. They are closer to me than many of my family. Whenever I have been able to participate in any of the functions here at church, I always seem to come away feeling that I have gotten much more than I have given. I am blessed to be able to work here in town and am able to have contact with many people from our parish through

my work. I believe that for today God has me in just the right place. I conclude with a note from Sirach 35:8-10: "With each contribution show a cheerful countenance and pay your tithes in the spirit of joy. Give to the Most High as he has given to you, generously, according to your means. For the Lord is one who repays, as he will give back to you sevenfold."

In the fall of 2000 the Stewardship Committee had planned (1) to show a video on stewardship to each organization and ministry; (2) to promote a sense of ownership and assumption of pastoral responsibility among parishioners; (3) to include the financial offerings at the offertory of Mass so that they are clearly seen as gifts along with the bread and wine; (4) to publish in the Sunday bulletin "faith stories" illustrating the themes of stewardship as it impacts people's lives.

In a phone conversation, Joe and Esther Martinez pointed to "generational differences" that had begun to emerge as younger Spanish-speakers became fluent in English. "They become more conscious of their role in the parish and are more willing to get involved. We will see a lot from them on behalf of our parish in coming months and years."

In Retrospect

Corpus Christi provides an excellent example of a parish profiting greatly from a strong diocesan stewardship education and support program. Firm episcopal leadership made it clear that pastors were expected to attend initial stewardship presentations, as Father Stier's account indicates. Furthermore, Bishop Cummings reiterated his endorsement of a stewardship approach during a visit to Corpus Christi. But the process did not flow just "from the top down." Within the parish vital Small Faith Communities, also initially promoted by the diocese, were generating a core of active, committed Catholics prepared to hear and discuss the message of stewardship with its focus of taking responsibility for financial and ministry support. The Garcia and Martinez couples were only too ready to respond to a call for leadership formation within both the diocese and the parish, developing a sense of ownership—this was "their parish"—and wishing to see fellow parishioners join them in this vision.

Corpus Christi demonstrates, too, the combined power that results from integrating two paths to parish renewal: Small Faith Communities together with adoption of a stewardship approach. Stewardship theology and practices were discussed within the communities, and the latter generated new ideas for ministry outreach which the Stewardship Committee helped publicize and for which "time and talent" were recruited, particularly at Ministry Fairs. These two approaches in combination account for much of the dynamism at Corpus Christi.

Stewardship always grows within a particular parish history and context and will be "stamped" by these factors. Corpus Christi has always been comprised of Anglos and Latinos, English-speaking and Spanish-speaking. Recent immigration has accentuated a sense of difference, with a Spanish Mass celebrated by the pastor being simultaneously an invitation to full participation on the part of Spanish-speaking parishioners and yet, as an unintended consequence, a source of uneasiness, even resentment, among some parishioners. Parish leaders, sensitive to this situation, decided to soft-pedal emphasis on the treasure dimension of stewardship, fearing that this would make Spanish-speaking parishioners uncomfortable, again perhaps even resentful, and hinder their full integration into the parish. Many of the newer immigrants had never been asked in Mexico to support a parish through direct donations of money.

Thus there evolved the strategy, supported by bicultural leadership, of stressing the time and talent dimension of stewardship, with the assumption that as volunteering for ministries increased, financial support would follow. Father Stier disagreed at the time. Like most pastors, he was acutely conscious of the need for an income adequate to meet budgetary needs as the parish continued to grow. The conflict never took an acrimonious turn, and one could argue that it provided a healthy tension in which each "side" came to understand that both ministries and income had to grow to meet parish needs.

Out of this context a sort of tacit division of labor grew. The Stewardship Committee took upon itself a creative implementation of a diocesan-recommended Ministry Fair, which turned out to be a distinctive success in publicizing the array of ministries (surprising many parishioners!) and recruiting new volunteers. Father Stier took responsibility for the challenging task of talking directly about money during the annual fall appeal. His frank approach, including personal disclosure of his own financial contribution, gained him much praise from parishioners. Giving increased substantially. In addition, moving testimony from lay witnesses reinforced his appeal.

Challenges, of course, remain. Getting more parishioners to pledge is a key to increasing the stewardship of treasure, but pledging is difficult for growing families, particularly if their incomes are modest, since expenses are often unpredictable throughout the year. The wholehearted volunteerism at Corpus Christi is admirable, and a sense of ownership and responsibility is growing, but new outreach ministries seem needed to address any notable increase in those willing to serve. The parish found in their Small Faith Communities an effective means of generating just such new ministries.

Working its way through these challenges, Corpus Christi somewhat painfully but effectively has come to reflect the stewardship promotion ideals set down by the American bishops in their *Stewardship and Development in Catholic Dioceses and Parishes: Resource Manual*, which followed publication of their 1993 pastoral letter on stewardship. Father Stier indeed exhibited leadership through personal witness, reinforced by a committed team of lay leaders. Communication of stewardship ideals was growing, and plans for 2000–2001 held promise of emphasizing them yet more. Finally, with regard to "stewardship essentials," a resounding positive response can be given to the bishops' question, "Are gifts of time and talent really welcome, or does the parish or diocese unwittingly send a message that it cares only about money?"[4]

Corpus Christi is a parish committed not only to growing a solid base for its own organizational well-being—a reliable financial footing, developing into a true community that learns to cherish its diversity—but also wanting to grow in service to the surrounding community as its ministry outreach expands—truly "the Body of Christ" in action, as its name indicates.

---

[4] Ad Hoc Committee on Stewardship, National Conference of Catholic Bishops, *Stewardship and Development in Catholic Dioceses and Parishes: Resource Manual* (Washington, D.C.: United States Catholic Conference, 1996) 17.

Chapter 2

Caring Enough to Make a Difference

St. Peter Catholic Church
Kirkwood, Missouri

The beautifully blended voices of St. Peter's parish choir distracted my search for a pew at the 9:00 A.M. Sunday Mass. The blues and reds of the stained-glass windows sparkled brightly in the sunshine of an unexpectedly cool August morning when I visited the parish in 1999. "See the elderly gentleman sitting up there in the front pew? He designed those windows," whispered Kevin Conway, one of my hosts. Evidence of parishioner creativity was visible throughout St. Peter Church. Walking through the vestibule after Mass was over, several full-color, professional-quality posters caught my eye: "Living Stewardship—Many Gifts . . . the Same Spirit"; "Living Stewardship—Caring Enough to Make a Difference." Graphic artist Jim Richter, another of my hosts, had designed and produced them. Hearing me comment to Kevin on their quality, one church member said to me, "New ideas in an old parish."

St. Peter's is certainly a well-established church. Jesuit Father Peter Verhaegen laid the cornerstone of the first St. Peter Church in Kirkwood, Missouri, in August 1832, founding St. Louis County's second Catholic church. Soon after, the parish opened St. Peter School, which flourished under the direction of a group of Franciscan sisters, and later under the Ursulines and Sisters of Mercy. Irish and English pioneer families made up St. Peter's first parishioners. Some of their names—Holmes, Sappington, Dougherty—are still on the parish roster,

19

though they are well supplemented today by the names of German and Italian families that arrived in Missouri during later periods of immigration. Built in 1953, the church I had admired at Mass is the fourth to house St. Peter's congregation, reflecting the long and steady growth of a parish that had reached almost two thousand families in 1999.

Kirkwood became a railroad town in 1853, thanks to five acres of parish land sold by Archbishop Peter Kenrick as right-of-way to the railroad company. The community flourished as the first stop for passengers on trains traveling west from St. Louis. Even today, despite its proximity to urban St. Louis, Kirkwood evokes vivid images of the quiet gentility of small-town Midwestern life similar to those found in Garrison Keillor's essays. Several of my interviewees asserted that while the St. Louis area attracts many young people who were born and raised in Kirkwood but left Missouri during their college years, they return later as adults to marry and raise children. As one parishioner proudly commented to me, "This is still a solid community where families and kids thrive and the schools are good."

Kirkwood's business brochure is similarly enthusiastic about the town's virtues:

> Kirkwood has kept things simple: insulated but not isolated (it's easily accessible to every major highway and interstate in St. Louis); and citified its community without sacrificing its charm: no parking meters, no factories, no Olympic-sized malls with miles to walk or winding ramps for cars. . . . It's a city that has mastered the art of modern living . . . Gift shop boutiques and classic antiques, kitchenware and ethnic fare, harvest grain breads and hand-me-down threads—the city has settled in nicely to the 90s. It's revitalized and energized itself with 29,000 residents and 300 businesses united under thousands of roofs by an infectious spirit called community pride.

Like the town of Kirkwood, St. Peter Church has taken pains to modernize its facilities, creating a pleasant, family-friendly environment for worship. A parish center was completed in 1981. A few years later a maintenance building went up, followed in the mid-1990s by a remodeled eucharistic chapel, reconciliation rooms, a crying room, a redesigned choir area, an enhanced sound system, and handicapped-accessible restrooms. I was visiting a "parish plant" that had been gracefully renewed for its next century, but as I was to discover, renewal at St. Peter's came neither immediately nor easily.

The First Phase of Stewardship:
Shouldering a Burden, 1989–1997

The story of St. Peter's transition to a stewardship parish provides a vivid illustration of the fact that in many parishes the decision to undertake stewardship is often motivated by financial issues. However, in the course of doing so, it is not unusual for a parish to find itself transformed in unexpected ways, far beyond immediate financial concerns.

In St. Peter's case, the transition to stewardship was spurred in the 1980s by a difficult and sensitive financial problem: maintaining St. Peter School as a tuition-free, parochial institution in the face of rising educational costs. In most regions of the country, today's typical parochial school relies almost wholly on tuition to meet its operational costs, and not infrequently parochial school can cost families $3,000 per child each school year. Well into the 1990s, however, many parochial schools in St. Louis clung to a long-standing tradition that parishes should provide full support for their schools. In a practice that reflects the Catholic Church's historic and important role as the primary provider of education to immigrants and their children, many schools in the area did not require families to pay tuition costs.

For much of St. Peter's school history, the contributions of churchgoers had enabled the parish to provide tuition-free Catholic education. Although all parish members were reminded to consider the school's needs in their weekly contributions, leaders had traditionally encouraged parents with school-aged children to be particularly generous givers. Some parents were less generous than others, but the overall rate of contributions enabled the school to maintain a respectable financial balance well into the 1980s. Critical to the school's financial health, of course, was the service of the teaching nuns, who traditionally ran the school and educated its pupils at minimal cost to the parish.

In the late 1980s, however, the entire nation saw a sharp decline in the ranks of teaching nuns due to retirement, slowing recruitment, and sisters leaving the convent. Not surprisingly, salary costs at St. Peter School soon began to escalate, and the school experienced financial troubles as administrators were forced to hire salaried lay teachers at far greater expense to the parish. A tight school budget meant that these lay recruits were markedly underpaid compared with their counterparts in neighboring public schools, making it difficult to recruit and retain a stable teaching staff.

Inevitably, the parish began experiencing strong pressure to change its educational policy and begin charging parish families for tuition. Rather than take this difficult step, however, St. Peter Parish in 1989 decided to implement a stewardship approach being sponsored by the Office of Stewardship Development (OSD) of the Archdiocese of St. Louis. Stewardship offered a way to cultivate stronger ties between parishioners and St. Peter Church. It had the potential not only to revitalize parishioners' commitment to St. Peter Church but also to increase parish revenues, some of which could be directed to the school.

To implement the stewardship program at St. Peter's, organizers relied heavily on strategies suggested by the Archdiocese's Office of Stewardship Development. One suggestion was that stewardship be clearly differentiated from traditional fund-raising, and so the parish chose not to focus too intently on the treasure aspect of stewardship. Instead, the program emphasized an appeal for volunteers to offer their time, talent, *and* treasure to various activities. To ensure that the new effort was well integrated into the parish, a Stewardship Commission was created whose chair would sit on the Parish Council, facilitating communication between the two organizations.

To popularize the stewardship program, the Stewardship Commission placed inserts in the parish bulletin, inviting parish members to service. As a supplement to the bulletin, the commission started publishing an occasional *Three T Newsletter,* emphasizing the importance of offering one's gifts in the service of others and suggesting opportunities for doing so. To further advertise St. Peter's volunteer organizations, the Stewardship Commission started an annual Stewardship Sunday in February, on which a Festival of Ministries showcased the parish's many groups and ministries. Motivation to participate was provided by lay witnesses—couples, individuals, and families—who took the pulpit on Stewardship Sunday to describe their commitment to giving and to encourage others to follow suit. The following excerpt from a talk by a lay witness in 1991 nicely illustrates the parish's low-key approach to stewardship:

> How much should you give? In the traditional sense of tithing, stewardship is not a tithing program. Each of us determines in a responsible and conscientious manner what percentage of his or her income is to be given off the top to God who loves a cheerful giver. . . . Stewardship also includes the gift of time and talent, not only to the church but also to other organizations, to our com-

munity. The parish catalogue lists the organizations and groups to which we can contribute our time and talent. . . . Another advantage of volunteering is getting to know and becoming friends with other parishioners. You will be surprised at how many dedicated people there are. Volunteering gives one an insight into the problems facing the parish and other parishioners. Suggestions for solving them are needed. You may have the answer. Instead of saying, "they do this, they do that," you can say, "we do this, we do that."

Just after Stewardship Sunday, the Stewardship Commission mailed a motivational packet to parishioners' homes. The packet included a letter from the pastor asking parishioners to prayerfully consider their God-given gifts of life, faith, family, health, work, and income, together with talents and time available for volunteer service. A personal pledge card accompanied the letter. Parishioners were asked to use the card to offer time and talent to parish organizations and to make a commitment to support the parish financially during the coming year. The pastor personally sent a letter of acknowledgment to parishioners who had returned the pledge cards, thanking them for their commitment to giving, while representatives of parish organizations quickly contacted those parishioners to encourage them to fulfill their pledges of volunteer time. In addition, members of the Stewardship Commission made follow-up calls to parishioners who had not returned pledge cards.

St. Peter's implementation strategy was effective. Parishioner support for the effort was evident in terms of financial support for the parish as well as a willingness to volunteer time and talent for church activities. Organizations and ministries began to thrive as active individuals and families joined them. In addition, many of the volunteers were young and new to the parish, bringing vigor to the St. Peter community.

However, stewardship became more complicated in the mid-1990s as the issue of a tuition-supported parochial school once again emerged. In 1994, St. Peter's welcomed a new pastor, Fr. John Brennell, who brought with him a great deal of experience in implementing stewardship programs in other parishes. Complementing Father Brennell's expertise in stewardship programs was that of the parish's associate pastor, Fr. Michael Boehm, who had worked closely with both Stewardship and Finance Commissions in St. Louis and had also served on the Archdiocesan Stewardship and Development Council.

Father Brennell recalled that not long after he came to St. Peter Parish the members of the Stewardship Commission began raising difficult questions about the relationship between the stewardship program and the school:

> When I came here, Stewardship Commission members took the stance, shared by many, that if we're all good and generous stewards, we could keep a tuition-free school. That was pretty strong motivation for some members to keep stewardship in front of parishioners, especially through the *Three T Newsletter*. And it was not only that the economics of running a Catholic school kept changing, exerting pressure to be generous with giving, but those with children in the school also appreciated the tax-break aspect of the arrangement. I hadn't been here very long when members of the Stewardship Commission began asking whether people really understood stewardship in its true meaning, or were they just sort of pledging tuition so they could take a tax break, with their contribution to the parish covering educational expenses? That's where the waters were getting muddied.

Both Father Brennell and Father Boehm were aware that the parish's initial decision to embark on a stewardship program was driven, at least in part, by the school's financial difficulties. The priests recognized that this situation had the potential to undermine the emergence of a truly spirited stewardship program in the parish. As Father Boehm explained: "No doubt that the former pastor saw stewardship as a way of preserving a tuition-free school, but that didn't prevent questions from being asked as to why everyone had to support the school to the same degree."

By 1998 increasing financial costs, as well as questions about the appropriateness of using stewardship as a means of financial support for the school, had motivated the parish leadership to announce that the parish would begin charging parish families for tuition. In doing so, however, stewardship at St. Peter Parish faced a new challenge: how to clearly separate the spiritual importance of stewardship from school support in the minds of parishioners so that the stewardship program could continue to expand. After all, parishioners had been urged through the years to be especially generous in support of the school. As Father Boehm remembered:

> A new challenge arose: People had to be reminded that it's an issue of overall giving, not just for the school. Stewardship had to go be-

yond school support. And not just in terms of money, either. . . .
We had to keep the stewardship message out there and not give up
on it.

To which Father Brennell added:

> We had to separate school support from overall parish support and
> say, yes, to have a full-time school the parish should subsidize it to
> a major degree (which we still do), but parents should bear a large
> brunt of the cost. Any help we emphasize should be for parents who
> do have a financial need, the ones who truly need tuition money.

Nevertheless, shifting to a tuition-supported school put Father
Brennell, Father Boehm, and the Stewardship Commission in the awk-
ward position of having to ask parishioners for more money at a time
when the tuition-free parochial school was being phased out. Among
parishioners, the school was commonly considered a primary motivation for financial generosity, the broader appeals of the Stewardship
Commission notwithstanding. Moreover, throughout the late 1980s and
early 1990s, the parish had been asking parishioners to contribute money
to capital campaigns for renewal of the church's aging facilities. "Why
should we be asked to contribute *more now*?" was a widely shared attitude among parish members. Not surprisingly, this reaction was even
stronger among the parents of parochial school students; they were
being forced to adjust family budgets to pay the new tuition charges.

The consequence of implementing a tuition program while maintaining a stewardship program is reflected in the pattern of pledging
from 1997 to 1999. As Table 1 on page 26 demonstrates, St. Peter's enjoyed a 50 percent response rate to pledge cards distributed to parishioners in 1997, just prior to the tuition increase. In that time period,
two-thirds of those pledging *increased* their amounts over the previous
year, while only one-quarter *decreased* the amount they pledged.

During 1998, the first year of the tuition charges, the Stewardship
Commission very effectively communicated that continued donations
of treasure would be critical in ensuring that St. Peter's other ministries
and organizations would not suffer. In response to this message,
average weekly giving actually jumped to a record high of $27,100.
Although the total percentage of parishioners making pledge commitments decreased slightly in 1998, this decline was offset by the 74
percent of parishioners who *increased* their weekly contributions in
response to the Stewardship Commission's appeal.

In 1999, however, we see a different story emerge. The parish could not escape the financially depressing effect of charging tuition for St. Peter School. School families, of course, were hardest hit, although the drop in giving was apparent throughout the parish. In 1999 less than half of the pledge cards sent to parishioners were returned to the parish, and the number of parishioners increasing their annual pledge amounts fell 7 percent from the previous year, while the number of parishioners who actually *decreased* their pledge amounts rose by 6 percent. In short, more parishioners were giving less money to St. Peter Parish, so the projected average weekly parish income fell below its 1997 level to $23,869.

TABLE 1

Pledging Patterns at St. Peter Parish—1997 to 1999

Pledging Data	1997	1998	1999
% Pledges Returned	50%	47%	41%
% Increasing Pledge	68%	74%	67%
% Decreasing Pledge	25%	20%	26%
Weekly Income Average	$24,976	$27,100	$23,869

The switch to a tuition-supported school in July 1998 was clearly taking its toll on parish finances. For St. Peter's, it was more imperative than ever that the parish leaders find creative ways of invoking stewardship ideals in the community.

The Second Phase of Stewardship: Renewal 1997–2000

The tuition problem was an important factor in St. Peter's effort to revitalize stewardship, but it was not the only one. Even before the tuition increase occurred, Father Brennell and the Stewardship Commission had been far-sighted enough to see that the stewardship program was not as active as it could be and had set in motion a plan for the program's renewal. For one thing, parish leaders generally agreed that stewardship awareness needed to be increased among long-time parishioners. Moreover, the parish was experiencing growth, and new parishioners unfamiliar with the challenges of stewardship needed to be informed about the importance of giving time, talent, and treasure to the St. Peter community. The *Three T Newsletter,* originally intended to communicate this message, was only being published irregularly. Lastly, the treasure dimension of stewardship required a new message so that parishioners would more willingly provide financial support to their growing parish.

Successfully developing and implementing a renewal plan would require creative thinking and strategizing to capture parishioners' imagination. Father Brennell and Father Boehm were aware that St. Peter's was filled with talented, well-educated women and men. While some were already in parish leadership positions, many others were not yet involved in the parish's efforts to invigorate its stewardship program. Perhaps, they reasoned, these individuals needed only to be addressed and invited. Accordingly, the Stewardship Commission quickly set about recruiting skilled professionals in the parish. The effort was successful, and by early 1999 a Stewardship Planning and Activities Summary could boast of the marketing expertise now devoted to stewardship at St. Peter's—diverse professional experience in public relations, marketing, research, graphic design, printing, video production, automotive and banking industries—all were instrumental in developing and implementing various activities involved in the overall effort to renew stewardship.

The renewal effort centered on a key assumption, one that had worked for the parish in the past, namely, that greater parishioner involvement in the work of the church would naturally enhance regular giving:

> Our plans and activities were guided by an overarching goal: calling people to greater parish involvement by asking them to contribute some of their time and talent to a wider range of organizations and ministries. We also made a deliberate effort to highlight the Living Stewardship dimension of the activities performed by those organizations and ministries. Our hope and expectation was that increased donations of personal treasure would naturally flow from individuals who had increased their parish involvement and sense of responsibility to the parish community.

To fulfill this mission, the newly energized Stewardship Commission came up with several good ideas to promote stewardship, including a parish survey, enhanced communication efforts between the stewardship leaders and the rest of the parish, new approaches to lay witness talks, an annual Care Fair to replace the Festival of Ministries, and more extensive follow-up phone calls after the pledge period. Each of these tactics is discussed below.

The Parish Survey

An important first step in the renewal plan was to assess how stewardship was perceived and practiced among the members of St. Peter Parish. In October 1998, Stewardship Commission member Connie Krapfl, a marketing expert, designed and directed a telephone survey of two hundred active parishioners. The survey was intended to shed light on what stewardship meant to active parishioners, to understand how they participated in stewardship, and to determine what changes they would like to see in the Stewardship Program at St. Peter's.

Asked to state which single word came to mind first when they thought of stewardship, 19 percent of the respondents to the survey replied "money/treasure," while 12 percent responded "helping"; "time" and "giving" each represented 11 percent of parishioners' responses. The survey also revealed that many of the respondents were aware that the St. Peter's programs and ministries provided opportunities to engage in stewardship, and furthermore, 60 percent of the respondents stated that they were involved in some ministry or organization through the parish. On the other hand, however, 8 percent of the survey's respondents said that they "didn't know" what stewardship meant to them, while 40 percent of the parish remained uninvolved in any stewardship-related ministry. One-third of the active parishioners who responded to the survey could not name one parish program that they clearly identified as part of stewardship at St. Peter's. The report concluded: Considering that we have a thriving parish, the Stewardship Commission has its work cut out to encourage more of our dedicated parishioners to become involved in the many opportunities for stewardship at St. Peter's.

If nothing else, the survey revealed the need for the Stewardship Commission to revitalize its communication strategies so that more parishioners would understand and appreciate the importance of stewardship as an active expression of Catholic faith. As one commission member put it, "The stewardship approach was not wrong . . . [but] our presentation of the message needed a new approach."

Communication as Central Strategy

The renewal effort at St. Peter Parish was aimed at increasing awareness of stewardship so that parishioners would contribute more of their time and talent to a wider range of organizations and ministries. Effective, enthusiastic communication was critical, and "turning up the volume" became a favorite metaphor among Stewardship Commission members.

To begin with, the Stewardship Commission revived the lagging *Three T Newsletter.* The new version would be published regularly as a vehicle for the renewed stewardship message. The newsletter offered profiles of parish organizations; for example, one issue commended the contributions of the Women's Guild, while another profiled Room at the Inn volunteers, who provided meals and hospitality for guests at St. Peter's. It also focused on the contributions of individuals: stewardship witnesses, for example, or the team of parishioners that produced a video about St. Peter Parish. Photos accompanied the articles; in addition, inserts elaborated upon stewardship-related themes, such as the personal rewards of giving to others. The *Three T Newsletter* encouraged participation and provided announcements of coming events, as well as appeals for volunteers from ministries and organizations seeking to increase their membership. In addition to the newsletter, the Stewardship Commission made use of the St. Peter Sunday Bulletin to focus on a weekly message of time, talent, and treasure.

One of the more exciting results of the Stewardship Commission's communication efforts was a video entitled *Face of St. Peter,* produced by parish member and film producer Larry Eberle. According to Eberle, the goal of the video was to "put a face on St. Peter Parish . . . and succeed in putting a face on stewardship . . . by showcasing a sample of the many people of all ages who live stewardship in part through their parish activity." A valuable teaching tool for the stewardship renewal effort, the video provided parish leaders and members with an opportunity to convey their commitment to stewardship in a polished, professional medium. Watching the video, I noticed that the elegant stewardship banners and posters I had admired in the foyer of the church served as a backdrop for the message of sharing.

At the time I visited St. Peter Parish in 1999, members of the Stewardship Commission made it clear to me that they were continuing to expand their communication efforts. For example, one initiative under discussion was a publication entitled "That's Stewardship," which would profile individuals or groups in the parish that exemplified stewardship in some extraordinary way. Stewardship Commission members were encouraging parishioners to nominate candidates in a stewardship suggestion box or to call the parish's newly established stewardship hotline with suggestions. The hotline and suggestion box, of course, would also provide commission members with a valuable source of parishioner input to the parish's stewardship effort.

Lay Witness Talks

A diverse group of approximately twenty stewardship witnesses were asked to speak to parishioners, four to six at each Mass. Included were unmarried single persons, elderly single persons, high school students, parish school children, and young married couples, some with children witnessing together with their parents. Each witness spoke for no more than two minutes. Each was introduced and thanked by a member of the Stewardship Commission leadership team. As the Planning Summary expressed it, "To our surprise and delight, many witnesses received enthusiastic ovations from parishioners when completing their talks." Following the talks, the Stewardship Commission leader reminded parishioners to prayerfully consider their stewardship pledges, to complete their pledge cards, and to return them to the rectory by mail or in the collection basket at Masses during the next few weekends.

From a Festival of Ministries to a Care Fair

The Stewardship Commission also revamped the annual Festival of Ministries, expanding its activities and renaming it the St. Peter Care Fair. Rather than focus solely on recruitment efforts, the Care Fair's new themes included celebration and gratitude. As organizer Angie Payken explained:

We wanted to time the event close to St. Valentine's Day in keeping with the theme "Stewardship comes from the heart." This was to be a true celebration that was as much a social, thank-you event for parishioners, and their stewardship the past year, along with an opportunity for people to find out more about parish organizations and ministries.

As in past years, St. Peter's ministries and organizations set up booths to showcase their work. However, the Care Fair emphasized family themes too; the fair included carnival booths with games and prizes, refreshment stands, even a face-painting stand provided by the parish's Kids Who Care, a youth community-service organization. A young people's singing group entertained the crowd, while children and parents walked around carrying helium balloons decorated with a stewardship logo. To reinforce the stewardship message, the commission set aside a special room for an all-day screening of Larry Eberle's *Face of St. Peter* stewardship video.

A year later Care Fair 2000 attracted seven hundred parishioners and succeeded in recruiting eighty-five new volunteers for a variety of ministries ranging from eucharistic ministers and children's liturgy to Room at the Inn and the Women's Guild. Parishioners chose from sixty ministries and organizations listed in a brochure entitled "A Time to Reflect." Major headings are Christian Service, Finance Commission, Education, Maintenance Commission, Social Life, Youth, Worship, and Stewardship.

The *Three T Newsletter* affords perhaps the best idea of what is going on in the parish. Profiles of ministries, provision of stewardship messages and biblical passages, and advertising of stewardship opportunities on short and long-term projects are designed to keep stewardship ideals alive in the consciousness of parishioners. Typical is a 1999 newsletter " Help Wanted" announcement for the Helping Hands ministry. Notice how the stewardship ideal is woven into the message:

> Helping Hands is our parish stewardship service effort that reaches out to offer practical help to those who have experienced a death in their family. Helping Hands volunteers cook and deliver meals, arrange for babysitting, yard clean-up and other practical efforts to help parishioners in their time of need. This wonderful stewardship effort is in need of an individual to coordinate the Helping Hands efforts of our parish. Is it you? Please answer this important call to serve Our Lord and his people. For more information call

the rectory . . . a member of the Stewardship Commission will call you back.

Father Boehm acknowledged these successes but went on to underline a challenge common to many, if not all, parishes:

What often happens is that people get comfortable in the ministries and organizations they're active in. When new people sign up as interested in a ministry, you have to give them follow-up calls, say, "We got your card. We may not need you right now, but welcome, we'll get back to you." At first, we didn't get 100 percent cooperation from all organizations and ministries to make these calls. This means that people who signed up were saying, "Well, I guess they don't want me." All this takes place with the best intentions of members, you know, we have enough people. And so we don't need to bother these new volunteers. We had to talk about this and finally made it the explicit responsibility of the organization or ministry in question to do these follow-ups.

Follow-up Calls

In a new departure from the previous practice of phoning only those who had *not* returned their pledge cards, members of the Stewardship Commission in 1999 called parishioners who had returned their pledge cards, thanking them for doing so and expressing appreciation for their involvement in the parish and for their financial support. Terry Rock, St. Peter's finance administrator, described parishioner reaction to those unexpected calls as "very favorable, in fact, quite surprising to a lot of people."

Stewardship of Treasure: An Update

As of spring 2000, St. Peter's appeared to be on a financial upswing, indicating that the new strategies were bearing fruit. The Stewardship Commission had distributed to parishioners Stewardship Intention Cards accompanied by a chart showing income ranges and suggested giving percentages. A preliminary report as of May 2 showed pledging households returning to 50 percent. Projected weekly contributions rose to $24,721, still shy of the 1998 high of $27,099 (see Table 1, p. 26), but $852 per week ahead of the giving level in 1999. This means that the

1979 families or solicited units averaged $650 in *annual* contributions. Since national research in the early 1990s put Catholic yearly giving at $386 per household, St. Peter's parishioners were clearly doing quite well and were poised, I think, to do even better as stewardship efforts bore further fruit.[1]

Children as Stewards

I would be remiss in telling the story of stewardship at St. Peter Parish if I did not touch on a program of which the entire parish is very proud: stewardship for children, given prominence in the *Face of St. Peter* video. Linda Doyle, director of religious education, worked with St. Peter School principal Maureen Jones and Parish School of Religion principal Carrie Sallwasser to introduce the theme of stewardship into the religion curriculum of both schools. For the 1998–1999 year, the children were assigned writing and art projects expressive of monthly themes. For example, October's theme of "Respect for Self" ("I am unique and I am a child of God . . . what are my special gifts and talents?") was expressed through books, collages, and bags the children made. The theme for Advent was "Respect for Your Neighbor." The children were asked to place straw in the manger to represent "kind and loving actions toward your neighbor." In January each classroom created a poster to continue the theme of respect for life. February featured the theme "Respect for the Earth," emphasizing respect for property. The October quotation is representative of the energetic quality of the themes:

> We have four trees "planted" on the bulletin board in the intermediate hallway. Each tree represents different ways we show *respect for others.* One tree reflects making good or loving choices. Another tree reflects the idea of treating everyone fairly. Exercising self-control or patience is represented on another tree. The last of the four trees reflects the idea of service, of giving of oneself and one's time freely. Each day new leaves of yellow, orange, brown and red are added to our trees as our students display *respect for others* [in the above-mentioned ways].

[1] National data taken from Dean R. Hoge, Charles E. Zech, Patrick H. McNamara, and Michael J. Donahue, *Money Matters: Personal Giving in American Churches* (Louisville: John Knox/Westminster Press, 1996) 32, 49.

Just as significant, in my view, is a policy featured in the video whereby emphasis on winning competitively yields to maximum participation on sports teams. No child is excluded from tryouts, and all who want to, get to play. "Winning isn't everything" is expressed directly in a truly countercultural policy. Good sportsmanship is a parallel theme insisted on by coaches and their assistants. The roots of stewardship are thus planted and nourished early among the youngest of St. Peter's parishioners.

In Retrospect

The impressive numbers of active parishioners at St. Peter's are not due solely to enhanced recruitment techniques and clever communication strategies, vital as these have been. Father Brennell's early efforts at encouraging RENEW faith-sharing groups in the parish contributed to an enhanced sense of community among participating parishioners:

> Once people find themselves in a community they trust, then it's easy for someone to say, "Ever thought of becoming a lector or joining this or that organization?" On parish RENEW weekend, people who had not been so involved were invited to come. Afterwards, the entire staff brainstormed, asking who was on that weekend that's not currently active in anything? The idea was, let's contact them. Same process in lining up nominees for parish council: Who are those not yet active?

Father Brennell's desire was not only to broaden parishioner participation; his vision for members of both the Parish Council and the Stewardship Commission was that

> they be people who have the concerns of the parish at heart. These would be people willing to give time to prayer and decision-making, and not so much on monitoring activities of parish organizations, like "How is St. Vincent de Paul doing?" or getting a report on the Scout troop. After all, the Archdiocese has a long-range strategic plan. How about us? The question is, What is our plan for *our* parish five years from now, say, in the area of social justice? Are we doing enough or not? We need our leaders to think along these lines.

He reflected, too, on his exchanges with the Stewardship Commission, praising their creativity in the ongoing renewal process:

I told them, continue to be supportive of people in the parish who are already doing stewardship, whether they know it or not. *Name it for them*, that it's not just volunteering, not just being joiners. If we can help everyone understand that there are great stewards of God's creation out there—and they are everywhere in the parish already doing things—if we can keep all this in front of new people entering the parish as well as in front of older people who may have rejected stewardship, we'll be inviting people to think differently about their future. Maybe we ought to ask, are we aggressive enough with people who just throw the stewardship idea out— I don't mean haranguing people—but talk to them about it: Are you intentional about living your Christianity if you haven't done anything for your own spiritual growth in the last ten years? Here are the things we offer. Maybe become a bit more challenging?

Emerging successes are particularly apparent in the area of time and talent. Parishioner response to Care Fair 1999 and 2000 provides ample evidence. The challenge ahead, as parish leaders are well aware, is to "turn up the volume" where *treasure,* or financial giving, is concerned. Early signs are favorable. Parishioner giving is up. In the context of the booming stock market in 1999–2000, it is perhaps not that surprising that some parishioners pledge from stock holdings. This path of financial stewardship will doubtless be further encouraged, particularly if a capital campaign is forthcoming.

"Keeping stewardship in front of people" in fresh ways that stimulate parishioners rather than turn them off is an imperative shared by pastors and lay leaders alike. This effort at St. Peter's is linked with inviting parish members to a deeper prayer life, not least through the beautiful liturgies that are a hallmark of this dynamic parish. "A bright future" seems far from a cliché in this parish, for which stewardship is indeed expressed "not in a single action but in an entire way of life."

In sum, St. Peter's presents us with a parish almost perfectly situated for growth in stewardship practice. Its links to the Archdiocesan Office of Stewardship and Development through Father Boehm opened programmatic advice and resources for renewal unavailable in many other dioceses. The collegial stance of the new pastor, Father Brennell, invited the many talented members of the parish to bring their gifts together and to think through and implement renewal of stewardship, spurred by the shift to a tuition-supported parochial school.

We see the partnership model of parish governance once more validated: it truly unlocks the energies and enthusiasm of parish members already involved in the church and motivates others to step forward. If stewardship means taking responsibility for returning one's gifts to God, we see it flourishing where the members of the parish council and the stewardship and financial commission are urged to stretch their gifts in encouraging and persuading fellow parishioners to also give from their resources of time and talent and treasure. A sense of purposeful, intentional community arises among them, helping to engender a shared notion of "we can find ways to do this." It is remarkable that this spirit also embraces the children of the parish, stewards of the future.

PART II

Stewardship Under Way

Chapter 3

So Many Different Ways
You Can Give of Yourself Here

ST. MATTHEW CATHOLIC CHURCH
SAN ANTONIO, TEXAS

A membership of six thousand families marks St. Matthew's as the largest parish in Texas and one of the largest in the United States. Located in the suburban northwest of San Antonio, the parish draws members from both comfortable middle-class neighborhoods and low-income public housing. Latinos comprise about half the membership, very largely Mexican-American but in recent years Catholics of Cuban and Central American background as well. The church is easily accessible from downtown San Antonio via interstates and a main thoroughfare that runs right by the parish. This profile is drawn from my visit there in 1996.

Monsignor John Flynn served as pastor since 1981, when the parish numbered around eighteen hundred families. Under his initiative the parish constructed the first new parochial school in the San Antonio Archdiocese in several decades. Its current enrollment is approximately seven hundred students. Seven buildings besides the church itself comprise the "parish plant." These include the school, a gymnasium, meeting halls, and a St. Vincent de Paul building that receives food, clothing, and other goods for the poor. Attached to the church itself is a chapel of perpetual adoration open twenty-four hours a day.

As we shall see, parish staff and members feel very proud of St. Matthew Parish, and particularly of its strong tradition of volunteering. One cannot visit very long without sensing the parish's vitality. Just the fact that there are four Masses daily, at 6:00 A.M., 8:15 A.M., 12:05 P.M., and 6:00 P.M., guarantees that there are people around throughout the day. The parish office is open until 8 P.M. each evening. The vast parking lot testifies to the over six thousand people who attend Mass each weekend.

Knowing this, it was all the more remarkable to learn that St. Matthew's was served by just two priests. Father James G. Galvin was the assistant when I visited in 1996 and quickly informed me that the acute shortage of priests in the archdiocese made this situation typical of many large parishes. Clearly, the vitality of this parish is a healthy response to this situation. Without a laity deeply involved in parish administration and ministries; without the six ordained deacons, who assist in performing baptisms and marriages, among other responsibilities; without the large staff overseeing a host of activities—without these human resources this parish would scarcely function. The pastor and parishioners have formed a vital and responsive partnership, demonstrating the fluency with which stewardship theology can be applied.

A Pastor Ready to Delegate

Monsignor Flynn lost no time in praising the spirit of the Second Vatican Council as he saw its manifestation in the parish. What became clear was his conviction that the laity at St. Matthew's are involved not by default due to the priest shortage; rather, the parish is, in a very real sense, theirs. Stewardship responsibilities assumed by parishioners reflected Monsignor Flynn's conviction:

> I think we have to start with the philosophy that our churches belong to Christ, not to us. It's His church and He will lead it where He wants it to go. A big part of this is involvement of the lay people, one of the biggest blessings that has happened to the church. In many elements of what I call ecclesiastical life, there has been a basic mistrust of lay people. You know, "They can help, but we're not going to give them the reins." This is the mentality. What we have to buy into is this: a complete partnership between us. What I see coming is that the priest will do, more and more, what he can do uniquely as a priest, which is basically to administer the sacraments and say Mass. Then delegate the rest to what other people can do. Here the deacons can do baptisms, they can do weddings if there is no Mass. Of course, we are flexible at St. Matthew. We have a group baptism that includes a Mass on the fourth Sunday of each month at 2 p.m. But we're also open to conducting individual baptisms if people request them.

Stewardship at St. Matthew's, then, has a lot to do with the time and talent dimension.

> Involvement is the key. This is the people's church and they are the Body of Christ. They have roles to fulfill. No matter what our level, we all have something to give, depending on our talents, how much time we have and so forth. Contributing to the Body of Christ. I like to afford people the opportunity to use their gifts whether within the parish or in the community. Volunteering at the hospitals or even at another parish. It's all part of it.

This is where stewardship comes in?

> Oh sure. Over the last twenty-five to thirty years I have gone to a number of stewardship conventions. I have felt that impressing upon people their need to give—that it's an act of thanksgiving for what the Lord has given us more than emphasizing the needs of the church—is a much more scripturally based presentation than saying "Here are the needs of the church." Stewardship says we're giving generously in thanksgiving to God, and it's up to the church to do with those gifts what it, or rather we, want to do with them.

I'm told that once or twice a year you get up with the time and talent card in hand. You explain to everyone at Mass what the various ministries are and say something about each one.

> Yes. I think the personal invitation is helpful. First of all, we have a big turnover each year. And some people have said, "Well, I've never been invited to do anything." So I take this opportunity for my personal appeal asking people to become involved.

Rather than put it in the bulletin and say "Here's a phone number?"

> Right. I've found the invitation from the pulpit very effective elsewhere, so I always go back to it. And new people always sign up.

The parish does have an impressive list of ministries, classes, and so on.

> Start with the five different Bible study programs we have. We found in home visitations that quite a number of people were going to non-denominational Bible studies. That let us see what people want. So we started our own programs. We've had a very good response to them.

You're sensitive to what people want.

> I think I have to be.

The Parish Council members I talked with say you don't endorse a new ministry idea right away, not with financial support, at least. You let it run for a while and see if it picks up support. And then at the next budget go-around, you'll endorse it.

> I hate to be a wet blanket on somebody coming up with a proposal. At times you don't know if something is going to work unless you try it. So I like to give people the opportunity to give it a go and see if there is further interest in it. Start out on a limited basis, a trial period. If it grows, then respond with budget support. That's the way we started with Stephen's Ministry, where you are trained to be a one-on-one support person for, say, a shut-in. You would visit that person on a weekly basis, maybe write letters for him or her, give support. It says, "We're concerned, we're a support network." We have thirty or thirty-five involved this way right now. It's a two- or three-year commitment, so you keep training new people all the time. It was started by a Lutheran group out of St. Louis—a lot of parishes have it.

Looks like stewardship also extends to singles' activities in the parish.

> Oh, yes. First of all, you have to realize that there's a big population of singles. And all ages. So we accommodate singles with a college-age group, a thirties' and forties' group, and another which is basically fifty [years old] on up. And we also have a singles ministry of a different kind, for those who have gone through a divorce, death, something of this nature.

Monsignor Flynn was referring to New Beginnings, for those who have been through a divorce or death of a loved on. As he explained, "for people who have to start life over." Two counselors have responsibility for these groups, which usually meet in the evening.

Isn't that ministry related to the two full-time counselors you have on staff?

> Well, you can appreciate how great the need for counselors is in a parish this large. There was no way I could handle this myself, even with an assistant pastor. What I do now is screening, in the sense that when somebody comes in, I'll recognize the need and refer him or her to one of our two professionals. We decided several years ago that we should have full-time counselors and pay them professional salaries. This comes to around $35,000 a year for each, a man and a woman. We furnish offices and secretarial help. They collect insurance . . . and return it back to the parish. What this comes to is the parish ends up paying the counselors out

of pocket . . . around $10,000 to $15,000 a year, the balance coming from insurance benefits. The whole thing is structured so no one is turned down for counseling.

Another source of pride is the St. Vincent de Paul facility next door to the rectory:

It's a wonderful thing for parishioners to see poor individuals and families, some members of our parish, going in and out of that building, getting things they need from what parishioners donate. It also encourages people to give to the storehouse. In fact, if the storehouse is all out of certain things, like blankets in the winter, someone will stand up at one of the morning Masses and announce that fact. By noon they have all the blankets they needed.

Someone mentioned an Adopt-a-Family Christmas program. How does that work?

St. Vincent de Paul provides a list of individual families and their needs. All on individual cards. You pick a card. On it won't be a name, but there'll be, let's say, the husband's age, his sizes, his wife's sizes, and those of the children if there are any. Two or three Sundays before Christmas we'll have these cards in the vestibule to hand out for people who want them. If it's food people need, there's a deadline when the food has to be brought in. The Knights of Columbus then deliver the food and clothing to the people. Some come to pick everything up but some has to be delivered. It's all been very, very successful. Some parish organizations will assign themselves to the larger families or take two or three families to care for.

By the way, I'm impressed by what the Knights of Columbus do here. Your chapter seems successful in recruiting younger men. In many other parishes they all look sixty-five and over! And here they do all these service things. What I've seen elsewhere suggests that Knights are often kind of decorative with full dress, swords, and all.

The last three chapters of the Knights I've started, I laid down the condition that they be a service organization, not fund-raising. So last weekend seven Knights went on a youth retreat to do the cooking for the kids. And as for dressing up, well, I don't believe in it. All those fancy robes and stuff don't appeal to me. I'm a kind of nuts and bolts guy—show me what you're doing. And don't put any fancy jazz on it. By the way, it's the same with the Holy Name Society, a men's group. They don't receive support from the parish, because after holding a meeting with very little to report, they sit down and play cards and drink beer. My attitude is, if that's what you want to do, you can do it at home.

You seem to regard the role of pastor as a kind of facilitator, letting people take ownership and responsibility. But I'm also told you know what's going on and exercise some oversight.

Also accountability. It's a weakness in any system when people have been delegated a task and turned loose and there's no accountability, no reporting back what's happened. That doesn't leave an openness to come back and share what the problems are. What I do say, if you need to speak to me as head of an organization, we'll set up an appointment. Or I'll see you for lunch or meet you for breakfast. And a lot of times I'll run into somebody casually around here and ask, "How's it going? What are you up to these days?" Works pretty well.

Monsignor Flynn is also proud of Perpetual Adoration he introduced in the mid-1980s. A group of about four to five hundred people participate, so that there is always someone (usually several people) present in the chapel, which is adjacent to the church's main sanctuary, even in the early morning hours past midnight. If the number begins to go down, an appeal is made under stewardship for additional recruits. Each year on the anniversary of its inauguration, the archbishop comes to celebrate a Mass at 3:00 P.M. A guest speaker from the parish is asked to commemorate the occasion and make an appeal for new people to sign up. Prayer groups have sprung up around Perpetual Adoration, including a Miraculous Medal group and a Spanish-language group.

Time and Talent: Voices from the Parish

Parish Council members were high in their praise of the volunteer spirit at St. Matthew's. Parishioners, they reflected, are "allowed, encouraged, and guided" in the various ministries so that a sense of ownership "comes from the people who participate."

When someone burns out or something happens in their lives that they have to draw back, we find people just ready to step in and take it on. The idea is, you step back a while and we can take over. Later you find them returning. It's an incredible environment.

Another council member pointed to an awareness I had been alerted to more than once:

> I think, too, that there's an understanding that our pastor is only one person, and he's getting a little older. The parishioners seem to realize that our pastor must practically beg, borrow, and steal to find an associate pastor because there are just so few. So while the pastor sets the tone, it's the parishioners that are making it work. Father knows that he can't do it all. We have got to provide. You know, it's part of us. This is our parish, not just Father's, and he'd be the first to say that. Once again, that's the ownership we've been talking about.

All pointed to the variety of opportunities available to serve but also stressed that parishioners have to be made aware:

> A lot of people don't realize, unless it's been explained to them, how important it is to give their time in different areas of need, whether it be the senior group or mentoring for the children's group. There are so many ways you can give and all of it is needed. There's a place for you if you're young-unmarried, young-married, old-widowed, old-married, or somewhere in between.

One parishioner spoke of her involvement as regent for Catholic Daughters. "People come from all over the city," she remarked, "that want to be in Catholic Daughters in *this* parish."

> Now there are six or seven other Catholic Daughters courts in San Antonio, but they seem to want to come here. I'd like to crow and say it's because we're the best, but that's not it at all. There are beautiful parishes, churches, and wonderful people all over the city. This one is just—well, when people ask, "What parish do you go to?" You're kind of like a peacock and you go, "I'm from St. Matthew." Or someone will say, "Oh, you're from that parish," like they're thinking we're "that rich parish." St. Matthew isn't rich money-wise; we're just rich in people.

Council members also remarked that the parish exhibited "a very mainstream Catholic life. It is neither right nor left; it is very middle-of-the-road. It is not on the charismatic side, neither is it on the very, very traditional side. If anything, it leans to the traditional rather than to the charismatic side, though there are some charismatic activities here." As another council member phrased it rather strikingly:

It's a "Culture A," "Culture B" kind of thing. You know, from "Oh, they shouldn't do this in church" to "Well, why not? The Lord loves you 'however you are.'" That's on the liberal end of things. Then you have the "Culture A" folks, who want it the way it used to be.

All pointed to the key role Monsignor Flynn plays in maintaining the large corps of volunteers:

When we go out and solicit people's time and talent and we get someone signed up, that piece of paper goes immediately and directly to that parish organization. His policy, which we all know, is "I want a call within a certain number of days. I want these people contacted." And he follows up. "Have you called so-and-so?" He doesn't want those pieces of paper to languish. Every week I get a list from two or three people in the Catholic Daughters' box, people who've showed an interest. On the note is "Please contact them" within so many days. He doesn't have to call me back, either. Where there is not a problem, he doesn't bother you.

What seems clear is that stewardship at St. Matthew's is very strong on the time and talent dimension. Its members respond willingly to calls for volunteers, and there are a great number of organizations and ministries inviting them to participate. Monsignor Flynn provides a kind of firm but permissive leadership that encourages people to take initiatives; there is also an awareness, at least among the most active parishioners, Parish Council members for example, that they must take responsibilities because there are only two priests in the parish. This awareness underlies the sense of ownership (this is "our parish") that comes across explicitly in interviews. Stewardship appears less well defined in its treasure aspects. Those I interviewed about finances provided a comprehensive picture.

Giving a Fair Share: Parish Finances

Construction of St. Matthew Parochial School in 1993 cost approximately $2,700,000. By the time I visited in 1996, total parish debt was close to $2,300,000. The chief strategy adopted was simply to continue a practice begun in 1984 of asking parishioners to make a three-year pledge toward debt reduction. After three years (1987) they were asked to pledge once again, and this practice has continued. By the end of fiscal year 1996 (June) parishioners had paid just over $500,000 toward debt reduction. Regular and special collections for that year, together with proceeds from the annual parish festival, came to approximately $1,835,000. Thus, by the fall of 1996, when I arrived, the parish was beginning another cycle of three-year pledges. As each three-year campaign begins, those who have pledged before receive in the mail a suggested amount higher than they pledged three years ago. This situation has meant, as it would in many parishes, a year-by-year reluctance to press too heavily for regular collections in consideration of the debt retirement pledges recently made. As Monsignor Flynn indicated, no pledging exists for regular offerings:

> Well, we do recommend stewardship tithing for the regular Sunday offerings. And leave it at that. We ask people to make out a commitment card, but it's not taken strictly as a pledge where we go back and say, "Well, you made a commitment for so much and you're so much behind." We like them to indicate what they intend to give each Sunday. And then we send them a yearly statement as to what they have given. But there's no such thing as going back and saying, "Well, you pledged twenty dollars and you've given only fifteen."

Tithing so often comes up in the context of stewardship.

> Yes it does. Here we use tithing as the ideal criterion to evaluate what they are giving. The tithe, we say, is what the Lord set down in the Scriptures, and if they want a guide as to what they should be giving, that's the yardstick to measure from.

Members of the Parish Council told me that about 25 percent of families in the parish make the three-year pledge toward retiring the debt. These approximately fifteen hundred families are also those who are higher contributors to regular Sunday giving. Council members were not surprised that Monsignor Flynn said comparatively little to me about asking for money:

> In the fifteen to twenty years I have been here, he always finds one of us lay persons to stand up there and ask for money. It's part of his own pastoral approach, as though he's standing at the side saying, "Well, we need this to survive, but I'm not going to go out there and beg people to give money. That's something you should be willing to give because you have an obligation."

Another member commented:

> There are two Sundays in a row each year when we take up the
> archdiocesan assessment. This year it was around $73,000. The first
> of those Sundays, Father wasn't even here. The second, well, I was
> heading the campaign anyway, so I went into the pulpit and basi-
> cally talked at all the Masses. Then it was over. This way, you see,
> when people come up after the Masses, they're not going to hit
> Father over the head, and say, "Hey, you're dunning us again."
> And I don't get hit; I'm just the messenger!

Does stewardship get mentioned in all this? How does it fit in?

> Oh, on the capital campaign. John Finke, the consultant we hired,
> brought in stewardship along with the campaign. I think a lot of us
> didn't understand stewardship in the first place. But he certainly
> brought it in. It was a big mix, a multimedia presentation—video,
> mail-outs, phone calls, special meetings—a really well-planned
> effort.

Several people in different conversations mentioned the Baptist
minister from a church close by, a friend of Monsignor Flynn's. The
minister was invited by Monsignor Flynn to speak on stewardship
from St. Matthew's pulpit:

> He was good! His whole thing was, "In our church it's publicly
> known that we give 10 percent, our tithe. It's just as well known
> publicly that you Catholics don't! So what is stewardship? You
> don't know what it is, so I came here to tell you." And the way he
> explained it, it was really good. And Monsignor Flynn was right
> up there on the altar, sitting and listening.

Another council member followed up, "Listening, yes, but he
doesn't say anything except to introduce the minister. And afterwards
he doesn't say to the congregation, 'I approve of this or I disapprove.'
He just lets the seed be sown." Several persons echoed what council
members pointed out: Giving at St. Matthew seems to be a function of
involvement in the parish itself. The following account reflects this
process of discovery:

> Before my husband got really involved here several years ago, he
> would always give, but reluctantly. We're both retired now. So
> when he joined the Knights [of Columbus], he became more in-

volved with the ushers, too, and other things as well. By doing all this, he began to see the needs of the parish. It made it easier for him to give and give a little more than we had been.

In sum, a reigning philosophy at St. Matthew's during my initial visit in 1996 was that if parishioners become more involved in the parish—share of their time and talent—they will eventually give more. In other words, the stewardship of time and talent will yield a consciousness that they ought to give more, since they now see where the money goes and how it is needed. This is obviously a long-term strategy. But it seems to remain true at St. Matthew's that a relatively small percentage of families do a high proportion of the giving, a pattern shared by many other Catholic parishes. A member of the Finance Committee shared the strategy developed for the early stages of the capital campaign to build the school:

> We went down a list of people who gave regularly. Our idea was to try to make a cut at a thousand dollars a year. Then we tried to see how many were over a thousand, and it was remarkably sad. I mean, here we all were as a committee looking at this list. We had thought there were many more people giving because of the overall amount showing. It had to be a lot of people. But that wasn't the case at all.

Another council member said:

> I think that all parishes have cores. And that core of people over time becomes pretty tightly bonded. They stay bonded. And as the parish grows and grows kind of far beyond this core, then you begin to become something different. But you do have to make the core big enough for a parish to become successful, to grow and become active. Everyone in the core influences everyone else.

Parish Update: 1998–2000

Following Monsignor Flynn's retirement in 1998, Msgr. Michael Yarbrough was assigned as pastor of St. Matthew Parish. He lost no time in inviting a group of parishioners to join him in attending the International Catholic Stewardship Conference in September. By November he had organized a new Stewardship Council, making it clear that stewardship would receive explicit primacy at St. Matthew's.

In a pastoral letter dated January 25, 1999, Monsignor Yarbrough congratulated parishioners on their generosity and noted approvingly that "stewardship is alive in our parish." One of his duties, he explained, was

> to cultivate the ongoing growth of stewardship. Seeking assistance from a number of parishioners to help foster this with me, we have formed a Stewardship Council. The council serves as a focus group as well as a course for evangelizing workers who will assist you and me during our growth as good stewards of what God has given to us. The vision is this: Through such growth we will increase in faith and experience the heartfelt joy of giving one's time, talent, and treasure. The hope is we realize that *stewardship is a way of life*, not simply a one-time program or yearly campaign.

The remainder of the letter left no doubt that Monsignor Yarbrough, unlike his predecessor, would talk directly and firmly about money. Sacrificial giving was the sermon topic on the first of two Stewardship of Treasure weekends in February 1999. The second weekend, Commitment Sunday, featured lay witnesses and distribution of an intent or pledge card, together with a tithing chart, or "Table of Sacrifice," designed "to assist you in finding the level of sacrifice that you wish to choose for yourself and your family." Parishioners were encouraged to "Grow One," which meant locating their present level of giving on the chart and then to "step up one percentage for 1999."

Moreover, parishioners were urged to attend, on the Saturday preceding the second Treasure Weekend, a financial workshop for families that was headed by Philip Lenahan, founder of Financial Foundations for the Family, a nonprofit Catholic organization. The promotion of the workshop stated: "At the workshop, you will learn how to achieve true financial freedom while improving your marriage and your relationship with God."

Results of the new financial stewardship effort were positive. Before the current campaign began, average weekly giving as of June 1998 was only $5.97 per family, or approximately $310 per year. The campaign's first year saw a 4.4 percent increase: by June 1999 weekly giving had risen to $6.23; by June 2000 weekly giving had increased by 10.3 percent to $6.87, or $357 per year.

Planning for a May 1999 Ministry Fair had begun the previous fall. Parish organization and ministry heads were kept informed throughout early 1999 and submitted descriptions of their activities to the

Stewardship Council. The Ministry Fair was judged to be a big success. In a follow-up memo from the council, ministry heads were sent lists of those who had signed up at the fair or who had expressed an interest subsequently. They were to contact those volunteers immediately and "invite them to your next meeting, class, or training session. Timely, personal follow-up will benefit all involved in the stewardship of God's gifts of time and talent."

Mid-August of 1999 saw council members attending an all-day workshop at San Antonio's Oblate Renewal Center. The agenda included making sure the Ministry Fair received "equal time" with sacrificial giving efforts; educating parishioners about appropriate percentages in sacrificial giving; raising awareness levels concerning tithing; sharpening awareness of parish needs; developing a common vocabulary about stewardship; offering more programs, such as the family financial workshop; and widening opportunities for more lay witnesses on Commitment Sunday. Needing improvement, workshop attenders decided, was follow-through, that is, specific invitations for parishioners to participate in the parish to reach the previously unreached, reducing, if possible, the "10 percent do 90 percent of the work" pattern.

In his letter of February 2000 to all parishioners, Monsignor Yarbrough designated the two Sundays before Lent as times for emphasizing sacrificial giving and stewardship of treasure—"A sample Intent Card is on the reverse of this letter for your review. Also included is a copy of the Tithing Chart, moving toward the biblical ideal of 10 percent." The following September a Ministry Fair was scheduled to actively recruit parishioners' time and talent.

In Retrospect

Stewardship at St. Matthew's finds its main expression in the areas of time and talent. Most parishes would thankfully welcome its outpouring of volunteer energy, which generates such enthusiasm about the parish itself. As is always the case, pastoral leadership has played, and continues to play, a major role. Monsignor Flynn conveyed a strong sense of ownership to parishioners, instilling the idea that the parish was truly theirs to maintain, its mission theirs to carry forward. This approach freed him and his assistant pastor for strictly "priestly" pastoral responsibilities, such as administering the sacraments, visiting the seriously ill, and so on. At the same time, he held everyone accountable for the proper fulfillment of responsibilities assumed, whether as a member of the finance council, as an usher or ministry head, or as school principal, doing so in a way that let them know that he trusted them to do well. His openness to meet with his staff and ministry heads and members at any time was not lost on parishioners. He was respected and admired.

Stewardship of financial resources has been problematic at St. Matthew. The practice of repeated three-year cycles to reduce parish debt had taken its toll on regular weekly giving. Aware of the demands on parishioners' resources that the three-year pledging entailed, Monsignor Flynn was reluctant to press directly and explicitly for increases in regular giving each year. Members of the parish staff, parish council, and finance council appeared to support this stance (understandably, since many were presumably among the most generous pledgers). A major effect of this policy was the restriction of regular givers—those on whom the parish depended for regular weekly support—to a relatively small core (recall the fifteen hundred families or households mentioned above—only one-quarter of the six thousand families comprising the parish). Moreover, as the finance council discovered, the number of large givers, that is, donors of over a thousand dollars, was much smaller than they had expected. The "philosophy" behind this, expressed by many I talked to, was that over time the expanding corps of volunteers would result in raising the consciousness of parishioners about the need for increased regular financial support. Therefore regular giving would grow, though perhaps slowly.

In my view, this is a questionable assumption. The experience of many Catholic parishes that practice stewardship suggests otherwise. They stress the need for parishioners to give (often through yearly pledging) first, because they grow spiritually in doing so in the many ways provided by stewardship theology, for example, in a sense of thankfulness for God's many gifts. And secondly, the parish needs the money not just to meet its operating expenses but to support and expand its many ministries of outreach.

Complicating this challenge at St. Matthew's, of course, was the recurring three-year pledging to reduce debt. It absorbed the "pledging energy" that might otherwise have been directed into regular giving channels and understandably made the pastor and the finance council reluctant to discuss money from the pulpit. Lay witnesses from the parish or the visiting Baptist minister may have talked about stewardship of wealth, but in the absence of strong messages from the pastor, little sense of urgency was communicated about the needs mentioned above. Regular giving is not likely to be enhanced under those conditions.

However, things are now changing at St. Matthew's. Leading a renewed stewardship program, Monsignor Yarbrough has begun to talk directly about parishioners' financial responsibilities in ways his predecessor chose not to. Under the banner of stewardship, making use of Intent Cards, a "Grow One" chart, workshops for parishioners on financial planning, and homilies and written messages articulating a stewardship vision, he is attempting to make church members directly aware of responsibilities entailed by sacrificial giving and stewardship of time and talent. Gains made in per household giving are understandably modest, given the history of three-year pledges entailed in the capital campaign of the early 1990s, but year-to-year progress is visible. St. Matthew may be turning a corner where stewardship of treasure is concerned.

St. Matthew's is a splendid parish in so many tangible ways. One of my enduring memories is attending the 11:00 A.M. children's Mass in the auditorium the Sunday I visited in 1996. Carefully prepared and rehearsed, and with several hundred parents and others in attendance, it featured children as young as five years old doing readings or processing toward the altar with gifts in an overall atmosphere combining gaiety with genuine devotion and reverence. The overall effect was for me—and I was not alone—a truly moving religious experience.

Chapter 4

We Take Care of the Poor
Before We Take Care of Ourselves

St. Marcelline Church
Schaumburg, Illinois

The Catholic Community of St. Marcelline is dedicated to continuing the mission of Christ in the world by inviting all to an awareness of God's abiding presence, by sharing a common commitment to stewardship, and by celebrating God's love in prayer and sacrament.

The "common commitment to stewardship" in this mission statement has not come easily. As in many parishes, it is perhaps best described as an ongoing project with ups and downs. St. Marcelline's was one of five parishes established by Cardinal John Cody in 1966. As Father Warren McCarthy, the pastor, pointed out to me when I visited the parish in 1996, these were the first parishes built without a Catholic school attached. The area was and remains thoroughly suburban, with homes affordable in the 1960s for middle-class families that flocked to the area. By 1996 property values had increased substantially, elevating Schaumburg and neighboring communities to highly desirable, if rather pricey, places to live. Father McCarthy became pastor in 1976. By the early 1980s it was apparent that the parish needed to build a meeting center. The planned addition was to contain five meeting rooms, a large "family room," and a kitchen facility.

Parishioners readily acknowledged this need, but "the pain of trying to fund-raise money for it was just enough to make anybody want to quit. I mean, nobody was opening wallets for this and it became a very painful experience." So went the description of Pat Schiro, business manager, who came to the parish as secretary in 1975.

Hoping to find a way of dealing with this "painful experience" of fund-raising, the pastor attended a stewardship conference in Minnesota in 1980. He listened to Dutch and Barbara Scholtz present the ideal of stewardship, including tithing. Also on the program was Msgr. Joseph Champlin, who addressed the strategy of sacrificial giving. Pat Schiro relates what happened when Father McCarthy came back from the conference:

> Father would say at our staff meetings, "I think we're looking in the wrong direction around here. I think we should be stewards." He was reading up on stewardship and sharing that with us. But our first reaction was, "What a Protestant word. We don't want anything to do with that!" As time went on, though, and we began to hear more about it, one by one the staff was converted, like "This must be the way the Lord is calling us to go." We began with sacrificial giving but later got into the stewardship of time and talent—stewards of everything, our worldly goods, the earth, our fellow human beings. So we've been practicing it for a long time now.

The Giving of Treasure

By 1982, Father McCarthy was offering stewardship training to couples who were already generous givers to the parish. They were encouraged and instructed on how to give witness from the pulpit about their own experiences of sacrificial giving. Pat Schiro describes the impact of their witness:

> These were young families with young children. Hearing them really began my own personal conversion—you know, if they can do it, why can't I? So I began myself to practice sacrificial giving. The more I practiced it, the more it changed my personal life, my outlook on money, my relationship to God. In a way, they were more convincing than the pastor, because I thought, well, he doesn't have a family or a mortgage or this and that. So it was easy for him to say those things. But for these couples to get up and say, "Yes, we give ten percent, and this is why we do it and how we feel about it"—that was strong stuff.

Not every parishioner caught this enthusiasm, of course. Pat Schiro spoke of "some really angry people":

> We hear things like, "How dare you use the Bible and Scripture and tell me how I should be giving my money?" This kind of thing. But they were not the majority, and there weren't organized groups protesting. There were many individuals who wrote letters but didn't sign them, so we kind of ignored them. And within one month our collection doubled! But what these protests did do was to cause a lot of people like myself to go home and look up the Scripture references. And then you realized that they weren't making this stuff up at the pulpit. What I'm saying is that the conversion comes with the fact that you're hearing and using the Lord's Word. It's not a program and it's not a gimmick to raise money and you know, some of those that were the angriest are today the most generous. Father McCarthy said, "Oh, that wasn't anger; it was guilt!"

Ensuing discussion between the pastor, the staff, and committees resulted in a decision to communicate to the parish that the stewardship of sacrificial giving was the way money should be raised. Resorting to bingo and bake sales had a definite downside:

> We depended on these things for our salaries, our plant, and everything else. We said, "No, it has to come from the faith of the people." You have to be giving back to God out of gratitude, and the parish showed its willingness to increase giving. Then we took it a step further. We said, "With the money you've given us, we, too, as a parish can give back."

By 1983 the parish was tithing 5 percent of gross income, as Pat Schiro put it, "to the world's poor in the mission Church." Ten different missions serviced throughout the world by priests and religious women from the Chicago Archdiocese were selected.

> We had a priest in South Africa, a nun in South America, a Jesuit priest in Peru. Just some examples. We contacted them to let them know that we were tithing a gift to them. We've done this for years, rotating among them with money we give from the collection each Sunday. And of course, when they return to Chicago occasionally, they come out and talk to the parish. By now that 5 percent is up to 9 percent, and we hope to raise that to 10 percent. In fact, we just received an award from the Jesuits for giving over $100,000 to a

particular parish, Virgin of Nazareth in Peru. The only thing we've asked in return from the missionaries is that they write us every time they get a check and say, "We have received your money, and this is what we're using it for." And they send photographs—of the children, themselves, pictures of any construction they're doing, and the like. In our prayers each Sunday, we pray for the particular mission we're tithing to that weekend. Some parishioners have begun letter-writing campaigns to them over the years. And I know a lot of parishioners who send them extra donations from time to time. And many of our people also come by the parish office to drop off food for the poor. We have a seven-day-a-week Food Pantry. All of us feel good to know how St. Marcelline's takes care of the poor even before we take care of our own needs.

St. Marcelline Parish also adopted a poor parish in downtown Chicago, Our Lady of Lourdes. Recipients write letters of appreciation to the pastor and the parish, which are published in the Sunday bulletin. Typical is one from the pastor of Our Lady of Lourdes: "Thank you for your August Sharing Check in the amount of $2,394.45. We appreciate it. It's helping us make some necessary repairs. Thank you for caring and sharing. . . . You are all in our prayers and in a special Mass I offer for you each month."

As generous as St. Marcelline's giving to missions may be, and despite the initial doubling of offerings in the early 1980s, regular giving by parishioners has not been strikingly high. Combined Sunday, Holy Day, Christmas, and Easter collections went from $809,643 in 1994 to approximately $869,000 in 1999, an increase of slightly more than 7 percent over a five-year period. Moreover, both the pastor and the business manager remarked that out of three thousand households in the parish, perhaps twelve hundred are active, regular givers. Of these givers, five hundred or so "are really the top givers." Actual tithing (10 percent of gross income) is practiced, I was told, "by maybe fifteen families" (including the witnessing couples).

Two related practices are recommended to parishioners: (1) to work toward a full tithe, out of which half would go to the parish and half to a charity of the giver's choice; (2) a "step-up" approach, urged in many parishes, by which members are asked to raise yearly giving by 1 to 1½ percent. A "Sacrificial Giving" flyer distributed indicates, according to income brackets, how much in dollars corresponds to a scale of percentages listed, so if the household yearly income is $40,000, 2 percent to the parish would amount to $15 weekly. Three percent would raise that amount to $23; a 5-percent commitment would add up to $38. The lay witnesses I spoke with endorsed the step-up approach. As one said:

> When people look at that chart and see what their actual gift is, or has been, it enables them to say, "You know, I'm not far from the mark. Maybe raising my giving is a do-able thing." Taking that step seems a little more possible. And it also lets you know that if you get a raise, here's how much more you can consider giving.

Nevertheless, high giving is attributable to few parishioners, a situation Father McCarthy felt deeply about:

> I think we need to speak more strongly about what the culture is doing to people. Charitable giving has gone down for some time. You know, people tend to see their wants as their needs; they can't distinguish anymore. I really think there needs to be a pastoral teaching on, and formation in, the gospel and their lives, an interpretation to help them see. My own belief is that we are in desperate need of theologizing on this. I don't see the seminaries doing it. In fact, in some ways, we priests need to start analyzing our relationship with money first, and I don't think we can do it alone. I think the lay people have to be in on it too. In fact, I have learned more from the laity on this subject than from anyone else. I think of the couples whom I have helped form, the ones who witness from the pulpit here and in other parishes and have spoken about their own experience of committal. But when I've talked to priests, we're like children in front of this whole question of money and stewardship. It's very hard to crack because men by and large like to think that their masculinity is determined by how shrewd they are in the use of money. Money is a powerful thing. When I bring it up at priest meetings, all they want to do is tell me stories of how good they are at money.
>
> I've given the same talk for fourteen years at the national stewardship convention, and it resonates with priests because I'm honest enough to talk about how inept I am at raising money. And the deep internal struggle that goes with it. All I'm doing, really, is articulating what they know. A lot of priests come up to me afterwards and say thanks. This is because they all have all these fears—you know, they've been thrown into these positions of leadership, and no one wants to admit they're really befogged by the idea of raising money, how it scares the hell out of them, how they have no idea how to ask for it. So what they do is invite professional fund-raisers to come in for them, and they just sort of step back.

Stewardship can appear so successful when it is implemented, though. So why don't more pastors adopt this approach?

> Pat, I'm not so sure it's that successful. I have a feeling that after twenty-one years here at St. Marcelline, I haven't really begun. I mean, I've converted people, but if you look at the income of our people here—well, if you had a good social scientist go out and do a survey, we haven't even kicked the dirt, much less dug into this thing. If our people were tithing, or even giving, let's say, two and a half or three percent of their income, I'd have to get a Brinks truck to pull up here each Sunday after the Masses! Now that's one way to talk about it and measure the problem; the other thing is, when we get down to it, when we get desperate, we're tempted to pull out all the fund-raising gimmicks and derail stewardship!

Veteran stewardship pastors like Fr. Tom McGread at St. Francis of Assisi Parish in Wichita say that it takes at least five years to get a full stewardship program underway; the message takes a long time to sink in. Father McCarthy agrees: "Yes it does. That is certainly our experience here at St. Marcelline."

To let matters rest here, however, would be unfair to the parish, risking the inference that St. Marcelline's parishioners are ungenerous. A Capital Stewardship Drive conducted between 1995 and 1997 yielded almost $890,000 in pledges from over one thousand parish households, added to approximately $276,000 set aside from parish savings. While estimated building costs originally came to $1,500,000, project delays, revised architect's projections, and necessary construction changes plus furnishings resulted in total building costs of more than $2,000,000. This situation left a debt balance of just over $1,000,000. Servicing this debt absorbed around 15 percent of total parish yearly income.

Thus, when the parish finance committee "respectfully ask[ed] that you continue to sacrifice for the building project" and parishioners were asked to contribute monthly in "purple building fund envelopes," it is hardly surprising that regular weekly pledges and plate offerings rose only slightly. It is equally understandable that the pastor was reluctant to press parishioners to increase regular giving. Perhaps the finance committee expressed the situation most appropriately by concluding in their 1998 report:

> As a sacrificial giving community, we are called to be generous. Our community is blessed to have so many who have embraced the spirit of stewardship. Together we all face these challenges of

increasing our operating income, reducing our debt and providing for our future. Together we are building a new St. Marcelline.

Stewardship: A Vision Renewed

Following Father McCarthy's retirement, Fr. Denis Condon became pastor in 1998. He lost no time in reaffirming stewardship as the guiding paradigm for the parish. Every new parishioner received a pamphlet entitled "St. Marcelline—Our Promise." Its cover sets forth the distinct mission and special spirit of the parish and asks for a commitment. The central place of stewardship is unmistakable:

> The people of St. Marcelline gladly welcome you into our church . . . your new home. We are a faith-filled people who love God and strongly believe in a Stewardship way of life. Stewardship means we firmly believe all we have comes from God—our time, talent, and treasure, and as good stewards, we need to return a portion of the gifts God has bestowed on us back to Him. The parish of St. Marcelline makes a promise to care for your needs— sacramental, spiritual and personal. We also are committed to caring for the world's poor by giving a portion of all our income to local and global missions. What do we ask of you? *As a member of St. Marcelline, we ask that you join in being a good steward. We ask that you give of your time—attend Mass, receive the sacraments, be involved in your parish; share your talents—the special gifts God has given you; share your treasure—return a portion of what God has given you, enabling your new parish home to help you and others.* We are proud of our community, deep friendships and care for one another. We invite you to take an active part in this faith life. We/I understand what St. Marcelline promises and what is asked of us/me. We/I want to be a member of the community of St. Marcelline and will do our/my part. [Emphasis in original.]

New parishioners were then asked to sign their names, signifying that they accepted the responsibility of membership in a stewardship community.

Opening the pamphlet, a new member found three categories of ministries to consider—liturgical, service, and catechetical. Under "liturgical ministry" were altar servers—worth mentioning because families as well as men, women, and children were also invited "to assist community in worship at Mass and at special liturgies." Four choirs were listed, along with roles familiar in any parish: Communion ministers, lectors, cantors, sacristans. A bit unusual was a meditation ministry "to spread the ancient prayer of Christian meditation so that contemplating goes beyond oral and imaginative prayer." This reflected Father McCarthy's active participation in The World Community for Christian Meditation (WCCM), an organization headquartered in London whose founder, the late John Main, was an indefatigable advocate of contemplative prayer. The WCCM sponsors speakers, retreats, publications, and videos worldwide, appealing to people from a vast range of religious traditions.

Under the category "service," new members could choose from ministries such as St. Vincent de Paul, Knights of Columbus, and Holy Name Society. However, St. Marcelline's also sponsored a Funeral Luncheons Committee, whose members "help families at a difficult time by providing a meal after the funeral." Other options were a women's club that engaged in various forms of community service, youth and young adult ministry, welcoming, stewardship, communications, and ministering to the homebound, "to provide pastoral ministry to fellow parishioners who are ill or confined, and to their families."

Under the "catechetical" category, members could be involved in baptism preparation, adult or high school confirmation, marriage preparation, and religious instruction for adults and children. Volunteers were needed during Sunday Masses to instruct children who were pre-school through age eight about the readings for that day. Less customary for a parish was SPRED, a ministry "to bring the disabled person into the community of St. Marcelline by loving, caring, and sharing."

These time and talent dimensions of stewardship commitment afford a contrast to the treasure struggles. Everyone I spoke with was ready to praise the volunteer generosity of St. Marcelline parishioners. The familiar strategy of parish Ministry Fairs did much to bring service and faith-formation opportunities to parishioners' attention. Heads of the various ministries were urged in a letter from the pastor to set up a table for the fair. Pentecost Sunday was the day chosen. In the pastor's words,

> On this day when we hear how the disciples of Jesus were sent forth, we want to offer an opportunity of service to anyone who comes here to worship. By making stewardship of our time and

talent an integral part of our mission, we become a living testament to our faith. We make this a holy place when we serve one
another with love.

Booths for each ministry and program were set up under a huge tent in
the parking lot. Coffee, juices, ice cream, and donuts were served.
Sometimes clowns and balloons were added for a festive touch. Parish
staff were unanimous in commending the willingness of members to
step forward and volunteer at the tables. Even older parishioners and
retirees, I was told, found it stimulating to walk around the booths of
the Ministry Fair. They saw what the parish was doing, and as one
parishioner remarked, "It all comes to a great example of public relations on behalf of stewardship in our parish."

One-on-one asking seemed particularly effective. As Pat Schiro
put it:

> Just a personal invitation to somebody, "You know, you'd be good
> working with high school kids, wouldn't you?" For example if
> you're a Communion minister, you're asked when your group
> meets socially or for prayer to go out and encourage someone you
> think would be a good person to come forward.

During my conversation with Parish Council members, a man recalled his wife saying one evening, "The pastor is on the phone for you."

> I couldn't believe it. You know, I grew up when the church had
> priests and brothers and nuns who did everything. Why would the
> pastor call you? But here was Father Warren on the phone, asking
> me if I would run for Parish Council. Why me? I thought. But then,
> why not? So I ran and was elected and have been involved ever
> since. But if he hadn't made that phone call, I doubt I'd be here.

Another member added:

> I remember I got a call from a nun, the new director of religious
> education in the parish. Oh, I had met her before a couple of times.
> She wanted me to be one of the leader catechists. And I had said,
> "Ah, gee, I don't think I can really do it." But here she was again,
> "Please come to this meeting." So, you know I said "Okay." After
> all, this was a nun asking me to come! After I hung up the phone,
> I thought, she doesn't know who I am; what if she thinks she's

calling somebody else? I just couldn't believe she was actually asking me. I ended up going to the meeting and it was wonderful, and that's really, I think, when I was reborn in the Christian faith. Since that time I've been active in many ministries here and enjoyed every minute of it.

Pat Schiro praised the volunteer initiative at St. Marcelline Parish, noting the key role of the Parish Council and the appeal of stewardship in supporting the parish's sixty ministries:

Over the years we've continually added to our ministries. We have a wonderful Parish Council that works with parish staff in setting goals. We've written a mission statement, so we know the direction the parish is going in. Of course, you occasionally drop ministries because they no longer apply. Let me say that the people here give of their time and talent better than any place I've been. Anything you need, you ask and it's taken care of, whether you need a religious education volunteer or a catechist or someone to wash altar linens. With stewardship, our approach is not to say, "We need volunteers." Instead, "We have another opportunity here for someone in the congregation to serve." It's not "We need you"; it's "We have an opportunity for you, you need to give." The people here are wonderful and just come forward to offer their help in any way they can.

Lay Witnesses

Witnessing, as mentioned earlier, is counted on heavily to illustrate what stewardship can mean in parishioners' lives. Sharing experiences as a married couple, I was told, is particularly effective. The following tributes paid by the wife of one witnessing couple are a case in point, serving to reinforce among parishioners the sense that this parish is special, well worth the donation of one's time and energy:

When Jim and I got married, I was looking for a parish that could get me back to a time and place I fondly remembered. A parish that was a family and cared about those in our parish family who were less fortunate than us. Jim and I had been searching for a parish to call home. . . . We would spend a couple of months at each parish. We got so frustrated that we started going back to the city to attend Mass at Jim's childhood parish. Finally some friends of ours had

asked us to come to St. Marcelline. We said we would try it for a
month and see what happens. When we came, the warmth and
friendliness of the parishioners overwhelmed us. Everyone made
you feel welcome and at home. Within two weekends we became
members and started volunteering our time and talents. I became a
lector and was again bowled over by the warmth and assistance of
the lectors. Everyone was willing to help. They went out of their
way to make sure I was comfortable and knew what to do.

This approach, of course, also renders the congregation more recep-
tive to the call to be more generous with their time and money. Another
witnessing couple cited "three main reasons why we give of our time,
talent, and treasure." The first reason, and least important, is that it

benefits us. We're so busy now—I know I guard my time—there
never seems to be enough. But whenever I spend time preparing
for reading on Sunday or helping others, I somehow seem to have
more. Somehow I always seem to get back more than I give.

The second reason appealed to the notion of family, once again reinforcing parishioners' sense of community:

St. Marcelline is a faith family. And in a family, everyone must do
his or her part. We do some of that every time we attend Mass. We
pray together, come to table together, sing together, and profess
our faith together. This togetherness is necessary; the bonds nur-
tured through togetherness are part of what makes families strong.
But there is more to being a family than that. Each member must
take on responsibilities according to his or her own talents and
abilities. Someone must prepare the dinner at home, just as we all
must work and share preparations here at church. We all must
have our chores, but they don't need to be a burden; they can and
should be a joy.

Theological themes form the third reason. After appropriate scriptural quotations, for example, "Amen, I say to you, whatever you did
for one of these least brothers or sisters of mine, you did for me," comes
the linkage to stewardship:

As St. Paul points out, stewardship is not an option—it's a calling.
All of us baptized in the name of Jesus Christ are called to a life of
stewardship—giving of our time, talent, and treasure. We must do
this in a prayerful, planned, proportionate and sacrificial way.

They conclude their witnessing by telling about participating in a neighborhood revitalization project in the Lawndale area of Chicago. When they arrived, they were assigned to a team building a chainlink fence. Their narrative illustrates the highly personal, concrete character of witnessing talks and how a good story can set up a powerful conclusion:

> Well, Doug is an urban planner and I'm a researcher—manual dexterity is not part of our job descriptions. To be honest, I had never even thought about how a chainlink fence was made, let alone build one. Why couldn't we have been assigned to the clean-up team, painting team, or gardening team? At least I would have had some clue about what I was doing! But they didn't need more of those volunteers; they needed people to help build fences. So we did. Just don't get any ideas about trying to contract us out! But we set up more than chainlinks that day. We made stronger links to that neighborhood. We showed them that although we may not live in the same neighborhood, work in the same jobs, share the same religion, or even (for many) have the same color of skin, that we cared. That despite the differences we may have, we saw them as brothers and sisters—we saw Jesus in them—and treated them as such. When we were working, or rather fumbling, on our first fence, a group of neighborhood women were standing near us watching all the teams at work on an elderly woman's home. They said this was God's work. God's face. God's hands. They said surely God was there with them. And we know He was. But to help someone else understand that, to help someone else see God and open themselves to God's love—no words can describe it. We are all called to serve in this way: to give of our time, talent and treasure. This is fundamental to being followers of Jesus Christ.

The New Pastor Looks Ahead

In his 1999 "Report on the State of the Parish," it was easy for Father Condon to build on the strengths he perceived in the congregation at St. Marcelline. After praising those involved in various ministries, accompanied by a description of each and where the parish needed to strengthen its outreach, he evoked themes of growth in prayer and in the spiritual life, which he had made a fundamental priority in his pastorship. I think these excerpts clearly reveal the role of spiritual leader and "encourager" that Father Condon assumed in the overall context of the parish's stewardship emphasis:

> The soul of the parish is its *Spiritual Life*. How the people of God relate to God and to each other in Gospel ways not only shapes the people, but also can determine the future life of the parish as a whole. I'm happy to report that the Spiritual Life of St. Marcelline is healthy. Our prayer life takes flesh through our Stewardship program. From the monies collected each Sunday we give to those in more need than ourselves. We help support a Jesuit mission in Peru and a mission in South Africa. We also contribute to local parishes and groups in need. This connection to the poor and needy is vital. Without that connection we can lose the understanding of the Kingdom of God. And along with our Stewardship program we have our sharing parish, Our Lady of Lourdes. We need our sister parish to remind us of all the blessings God has given us. While there are lots of things to do and care for, my concern is for the mission of the Church. We are called by Christ to follow, that is, to build up the Kingdom of God. I'm concerned that we may not be listening to that call. We may not be hearing all the needs of the people or we may not be responding well to them . . . not hearing the call to ministry whether as Greeters, Eucharistic Ministers, Ministers of Care or other parish ministries. . . . Becoming mediocre is my biggest fear. We humans can easily become complacent about life. We can come to church and go through the motions Sunday after Sunday until it becomes just some dull routine. The only way we can get the fire for the mission of the Church is if we get to know the person who calls us. And that takes prayer. I renew my call for all of us to spend one hour a week in church in prayer. I realize this is a sacrifice. But the only way we get to know anyone, including the Lord, is to spend time with Him. And if we don't want to get to know the Lord, then why are we here? Without Jesus Christ as the center of our life as a parish, we have no reason to exist. We are not a social club or a welfare institution. We are a people called by Christ to build the Kingdom of God. St. Marcelline is a great place, wonderfully kind and generous people worshiping in a beautiful space. While we have a large number of people who volunteer their time, talent, and energy to our community and its mission, there are so many more who could. I invite you over the next year to get to know the Lord better through prayer, listen to the call He may have for you, and be generous in answering that call. I firmly believe that the Holy Spirit has great things in store for us, if only we will heed. (Emphasis in the original.)

In Retrospect

Stewardship has a two-decade history of emphasis at St. Marcelline Parish. Its primacy is evident in both conversations with staff and church members and in a variety of written materials. The forms it assumes are not lost on parishioners. Frequent reminders cite sharing with poor parishes and urge active participation; witnesses testify how stewardship plays out in everyday life; large numbers of ministry volunteers help to engender a spirit of enthusiasm that emanates from and contributes back to a strong sense of parish community and purpose. Warm welcoming of visitors and new members was frequently mentioned. One-on-one asking, whether by pastor, staff, or fellow church members, has been an important key in getting more men and women to volunteer for ministries and organizations.

All give credit to Father McCarthy, whose quiet but warm endorsement of stewardship and early training of lay witnesses were keys to launching stewardship at St. Marcelline's. He saw the need for a theology of stewardship, observing its potential for penetrating the resistance many pastors have to dealing with and talking to their parishioners about money.

Regular giving has not been spectacular, again underlining that stewardship is always grafted onto a particular local situation. While giving to the building campaign, proposed under the banner of stewardship, has been solid, the parish balked when it came to increasing regular giving. Both pastors have been understandably sensitive about pushing too hard, preferring an approach of prayerful reflection and persuasion. In fact, as impressive as any single feature of St. Marcelline's, in my view, is an intangible: pastors who have been especially appreciative of prayer and spiritual growth. Their convictions translate into an emphasis on the theological underpinnings of stewardship that comes across in sermons, Sunday bulletin messages, and annual reports. This dimension is immeasurably helpful, I believe, in enabling parishioners to view stewardship not as "just another way of asking us for money" but as a call to discipleship. This call takes seriously the return of one's time, talents, and treasure to the service of God and Church, with special emphasis on generous outreach to adopted sister parishes in Chicago and around the world.

Both in outreach to other parishes and in generous volunteering for ministries, St. Marcelline Parish is outstanding. Father McCarthy began the practice, which has continued through his successor, Father Condon, of personally asking parishioners if they would like to serve in a particular capacity. Both have couched their inquiry as "an opportunity for you to serve" rather than "we need you to do this," with an implied emphasis on giving of one's time and talent. It is little wonder that this parish engenders responses of love and loyalty among its members.

Chapter 5

Stewardship Demands Conversion

CHURCH OF ST. GERARD MAJELLA
PORT JEFFERSON, NEW YORK

Stewardship does not spring into being one fine morning because the pastor says, "We've started the program, everyone get aboard." Adopting a stewardship approach challenges pastor, staff, and parishioner. The American bishops warn against any sunny optimism in two trenchant statements:

> In the lives of disciples . . . something else must come before the practice of stewardship. They need a flash of insight—a certain way of *seeing*—by which they view the world and their relationship to it in a fresh, new light. . . . Christian disciples experience conversion—life-shaping changes of mind and heart—and commit their very selves to the Lord.[1]

Fathers William Hanson and Christopher Heller, copastors of St. Gerard Majella Parish, nodded in recognition of the bishops' wisdom. In 1990 they had inherited a parish of approximately four thousand families near the historic harbor port of Long Island in the Diocese of Rockville Centre. To say that St. Gerard's was in terrible shape financially is a woeful understatement.

Total revenues in 1992–1993 came to $431,670, or slightly over $100 per household per year. Expenses, on the other hand, totaled $541,767,

---

[1] National Conference of Catholic Bishops, *Stewardship: A Disciple's Response: A Pastoral Letter on Stewardship* (Washington: United States Catholic Conference, 1993) 41, 45 (emphasis in original).

resulting in a deficit of $110,097. While parish income increased by almost $4,300 the following year, expenses also increased, leaving a shortfall of $116,678. As we are about to see, a vigorous stewardship approach began to take effect from 1993 through 1995. Especially impressive was an increase in regular weekly collections (excluding fundraising from other sources). From $310,515 in 1993–1994, the parish funds increased to $370,818 a year later—a rise of almost 20 percent that closed the deficit to a manageable $15,000. St. Gerard's had begun to see daylight again, but the path to revitalization was by no means easy for those pastors. I share their conversion stories because in stark, colorful narrative they exemplify those enlightening moments of truth about money, moments known by virtually every pastor who commits to the stewardship ideal.

Conversion Begins at the Top:
The Pastors' Struggle

Fathers Hanson and Heller were remarkably open about their personal stewardship journeys through the process of reinvigorating St. Gerard's. "Flashes of insight" and "life-shaping changes" are indeed apt descriptions of their experiences. Father Hanson began:

> Financial desperation eventually got us thinking about stewardship. But we first started with a tithing emphasis. The reason was that both of us as curates [associate pastors] had experienced tithing programs before we came here. And we were inspired by them, I would say. But under the guise of not wanting to go too far too fast, we were kind of afraid of the whole thing. I mean, as inspiring as the tithing program was, there was something missing we couldn't quite put our fingers on. So in the first three years, as the financial situation got worse and worse, well, we knew what not to do: get up and rant and rave and scream and say you've got to give this much money. But bless him, Monsignor John J. Bracken of the Brooklyn Diocese, member of the coordinating committee of the International (then National) Catholic Stewardship Council, brought in the National Pastor's Stewardship Development Conference in 1993. And the bishop of the Brooklyn Diocese subsidized our attendance. It was there I first heard Monsignor Joseph M. Champlin speak about stewardship. Although we had used his books, I had never been a big fan of his and wasn't prepared to be open to what

he had to say. But Joe gave absolutely the finest presentation of the whole weekend. Oh, sure, the prior stuff on development was good, but it wasn't motivating; it was statistics. Then Joe talked. He was clear, distinct, eight points, right through. I thought, my God, now I know what I've been missing. To add to this, Monsignor Bracken knew what we pastors would need— not just to go home and tell our parishioners about this, but bring them directly to hear it themselves. He told us that we'd have a day the following March (1994) where we'd bring a group of parishioners along with ourselves to hear Dutch and Barbara Scholtz. The idea was for lay persons to hear lay persons talk about stewardship.

I was already hearing a lot about the Scholtzes in parishes I visited. They had become a veritable celebrity couple in their willingness to travel far and wide to talk to parish groups, often speaking at all the Sunday Masses in the parish they visited. Father Hanson asked his fellow pastor to help him find a dozen parishioners to go on the March weekend to hear Monsignor Champlin and the Scholtzes. Fr. Christopher Heller was dubious:

> Ask parishioners to go to a weekend conference on money? It was like saying, "Hey, you want to go down to the garbage fields and fight with the seagulls for food?! Well, I just happen to be busy that weekend, Father." We could just hear it. Well, twelve brave parishioners would eventually come. They heard the same excellent talk from Joe Champlin, but it was the witness talk by the Scholtzes that finally put me over the edge personally in terms of my own personal conversion. One of the Scholtzes' favorite examples is about this beautiful bedroom set they had set their hearts on for years and planned to purchase. They finally decided to forego it as a symbol of the consumerism they were leaving behind in the name of stewardship. They went from there to the idea that God loves you unconditionally. And I'm saying, yeah, I believe that. But what I was missing, I realized, was that if *we* don't love unconditionally, how can we experience God's unconditional love? The awakening was definitely emotional. There I was, totally convicted, hiding under my chair. For example, I wasn't giving *any* money to the Bishop's Annual Appeal because it was all going to Catholic schools—15 percent of our parish income. Giving that money was sinking our ship here at St. Gerard. And now I know why we can't make money move in our parish: I am treating the Bishop the same way parishioners are treating me. I recall saying, "Holy mackerel,

remember Pogo? I have met the enemy and he is me!" The ultimate miracle in this is that since my stewardship conversion started, I've never begrudged the schools a penny of it.

So that's what's meant by a life-changing experience?

Right. One of my classmates puts it very well: we live in a world of lack or we live in a world of abundance. He means, you either lack or you see abundance. In a world of lack, you fight over limited resources. But in a world of abundance, you say, "Oh sure, give them the money because there's more where that came from." That's a huge difference, you know.

I asked Father Heller if he went through the same experience. He cited the impact of the Scholtzes but added that his resistance to the stewardship of money went back to his first parish assignment as a priest. A couple from New Jersey was invited to speak at all the Masses about tithing. Heller acknowledged their courage as visitors in bringing up this subject to parishioners, but when the couple dined as guests in the rectory afterwards, the husband remarked that after doing tithing for a year and a half,

"My ship came in." And I said, "No, that's not it. It's not about getting paid back in our lifetime." In reality I was objecting for two reasons. First off, don't ask me as a priest to think about my own money, because I am already giving my time, my talent, in fact, my life to the Church. This money stuff makes me nervous. But secondly, the idea that you can have your cake and ice cream and eat it all now reminded me of huckster preachers. So my resistances were building. But to hear a phrase, as Bill said, like God loves you unconditionally, and what is your response—that begins to wear away your resistance. It begins to challenge me. How am I treating God, anyway?

Let me tell you my own "moment of truth": I love watching westerns. In this one the gunslinger was playing cards with these other guys at the O.K. Corral. They're having drinks and different guys are dealing the cards. And all of a sudden, someone's dealing cards from the bottom of the deck. He wins three games in a row, one of them with four aces. Hello! What's going on here? Something a little cheesy and suspicious about this. But when I saw this guy take that card from the bottom of the pile, it struck me—yes, that's what I was doing in regard to money: I was "dealing" with God, giving to God and the work of the Church from the bottom of the deck. I was trying to be underhanded about it, shielding what I had from God.

Here's the example I used this past weekend in preaching: We act as though that little folder that arrives from the bank with your checkbook balances comes with this Kryptonite seal. God can't see through it—as if God doesn't know where the money is going or as if, when I close my checkbook, God doesn't have access to it. Or I'm going to cut God off without an allowance somehow! It's just ridiculous, insane. The conversion that I had to go through required me to realize (a) that I could not use the priesthood as a hiding-out point, and (b) that God was interested in my money as well, and that my time and talent had to be balanced with the treasure. Otherwise there was something lacking, something missing.

Father Hanson picked up these themes and concluded:

You know, it's a good exercise to imagine the full dimensions of these defensive postures. When stewardship was introduced to pastors last year, I told the story about my attitude towards the Bishop's Appeal, that I was treating that appeal the way my parishioners were treating me. I told them I imagined one day this ridiculous scenario of the bishop going through all the checks coming in from the diocese saying, "I can't find Bill Hanson's hundred dollars." The bishop must be upset! Well, that scenario is so incredibly stupid. Who am I hurting here?

From the personal stories of Father Hanson and Father Heller, it was clear that the conversion by which they "viewed the world and their relationship to it in a fresh new light" made it imperative for them to commit to stewardship wholeheartedly first before asking parishioners to give of their time, talent, and treasure.

View of Church Members: A Parish Revitalized

Conversations with active members of St. Gerard Parish revealed their appreciation of the difference made by the two pastors. I asked Rosemary, a eucharistic minister: "If I were church shopping, came here for Mass, what would I find and how would I be treated?"

Oh, everyone's so friendly. First of all, the pastors know your name. That alone—when someone greets you by name, even the seminarian we had here for a while—that makes a difference. The pastors made a real effort when they first came. They'd ask me my name when I'd leave Mass in the morning; then they'd ask me again to make sure. A real effort. When you're called by name, you feel someone knows and cares. But other people are friendly too. When my mother comes here occasionally, she says she feels more at home here than in her parish, where she's lived for seventy years! People will smile, "Hi, how are you doing?" There are so many nice things going on. Before we redid the church inside, my husband, who is not a Catholic, would say, "Is this a gymnasium?" But if you're looking for external things, then true, you're not going to see the gorgeous things you see in some other parishes: traditional pews, stained-glass windows, statues. The parish where I grew up, it's not breathing, it's dying. You come in and it's many more older people. You don't see the young families as you see them here. Oh sure, it might be a noisy Mass for that reason, but it's life!

The friendliness and appreciation of parishioners appeal to the church-goers in this parish, and many attribute this to their pastors.

St. Gerard's has a core of parishioners who were present from the founding. They had become friends because as parents of young families, they shared many common interests. Penny is director of the parish Stewardship Supper, which serves around a hundred people every other Thursday evening. She recalled the original parishioners meeting in a movie theater before the church was built:

We called ourselves "members of St. Fox!" We'd hang out before Mass or after Mass in the lobby. It was all young families. So everybody got to know each other and become friends. When we built this church [we decided] to have the kind of lobby we have outside the entrance to the church itself. We wanted to have a place where we could still gather.

When the former pastor became ill, Penny said, "It had gotten very quiet" at St. Gerard.

Before these two priests came, [church life] was kind of slacking off, but they . . . put new life back into it and brought back the original spirit, actually. They renewed the old people and got the new people really involved. Stewardship has been like a breath of fresh air.

From what I gather, when the priests talk about stewardship, it's something they practice, too.

Financially they practice it, definitely. And with their time and talents, too. They're both very talented and allow us to share some of that.

So they're not asking you to do something they don't do?

No. That's an important part of stewardship. I've been involved in stewardship since it came to Long Island. And a crucial part of it is having a pastor being a part of it. If the pastor doesn't believe stewardship can help, it doesn't help. And another thing—stewardship isn't something you're going to introduce this year and then it's going to grow forever. You really have to keep after it. People have to be reminded all the time. First of all, remind people they themselves are gifts to start with—gifts to the parish. And they have gifts to give. Even when they're having hard times, something good is happening. You know, we overlook that good things are happening to people all the time. They just don't always look for them. It's a matter of priorities, looking for all those good things. Being pleased and happy and returning some of it.

The two pastors had no qualms about sharing their own troublesome stewardship journeys with parishioners, whether from the pulpit or in conversations. As Rosemary said:

They share stories with us from the pulpit about how they thought they were giving enough; like, after all, they're giving their lives to service here so don't really have to contribute financially. Father Bill told about a loan he made to a fellow priest. Father said, "Sure," but inside he was really waiting for that money to be repaid. And when he finally got into stewardship, he knew he had to let go. When you hear these two priests, they're not perfect, they're just like us and we're in this together. I think they've been really amazing at getting people to give . . . well, the money, but more than the money, to do things around the church. To identify the church, get involved in ministries—it's that type of thing that's really grown, involving people. And I think when you feel a part of your parish, then you're much more open to giving. And when you don't feel a part, then it's "They're always asking for money."

Penny was in strong agreement:

> I wound up involved in our Stewardship Supper. We've had our Thursday night soup kitchen for quite a while, but we renamed it Stewardship Supper. A small group of us started it years ago, but what we did was to open it to the parish, including our children, who can earn service time for the Christian Formation Program.[2] When the kids finish eating, the adults stay on. We're proud of having so many young men, young fathers, who work our kitchen every Thursday night. And they clean up as well as serve—taking down the chairs and tables and putting them back. Take last night: We had limited staff and the men said, "That's okay, we can do it." They love it. And they keep talking about it and it keeps growing.

Here is a successful example of shifting volunteerism to a ministry: a soup kitchen becomes a stewardship supper open to the entire parish for participation.

Lay Witnesses: Stewardship as Vital Conversion

Not everyone in St. Gerard Parish was new to stewardship. Far from it. In Lou and Ginny and Howie and Marge the parish had two couples for whom stewardship was central in their lives. Both couples were long-standing members of St. Gerard's. A few years after the two pastors arrived, the two couples attended the International Catholic Stewardship Conference, where they underwent a conversion that committed them to stewardship ideals. Contact at the conference with Father Tom McGread and members of St. Francis of Assisi parish in Wichita, Kansas, played a big role in this new commitment. They subsequently joined a team that witnessed at various parishes in the diocese. Marge's account forms an excellent example of how involvement in parish life prepares the soil in which stewardship ideals eventually flourish:

> As we became more heavily involved in St. Gerard, we began to realize that the church is people. A "church" is just the building where people meet. It is community. People and community. As I

---

[2] Personal conversation with Penny, director of the Stewardship Supper.

started to get involved in the parish, we all took part and became more giving of ourselves. We then started to realize what that really meant, that people are the church. This parish has supported that concept for me ever since we've been in it.

Her husband Howie echoed Marge's praise of the parish, noting how stewardship arose from this experience:

Since its beginning this parish had a family atmosphere. People were family. We know and taught people who are now married and have families. With some, we were involved in the baptisms of their kids. So it's really like an extended family. We know a lot of people personally and have been very involved in their lives. This has always been a very community-minded parish. You see, stewardship was just a confirmation of what we've been called to as Christian. The call is to discipleship. Stewardship was a reaffirmation of what we had already been involved in, giving back to God first fruits. It was just additional support. Now, it all started small. When we went to the national conference, we could only identify two other people from this diocese. That impressed me. I said, "How come so little from such a large diocese?" We sounded big horns when we got back. We had a recognition day for stewardship in our parish and invited other parishes to come. We did some witnessing and a lot of sharing. That came easy for us because we had been involved in Small Church Communities like those advocated by Father Art Baranowski [author of *Creating Small Church Communities: A Plan for Restructuring the Parish and Renewing Catholic Life*]. So there were a lot of people you could draw from who were already involved in ministries. All this made it a lot easier for us to get stewardship underway.

Marge went on to affirm her experience that the pastor's support in beginning stewardship is critical:

Oh, it is central, absolutely essential. If your pastor is not really for stewardship, it's just not going to work. You will not get the cooperation of the people. You need the pastor's approval and his conversion; then the people start listening, because they put the priest on a pedestal so much. In fact, they look up to him for everything instead of looking to the Body of Christ, which is where everything really needs to come from.

Let me share something. Someone gave me a bulletin from another parish with a story from the pastor. Apparently some lay people did their witnessing for stewardship and everything went well. The pastor wrote that he understood and thanked people for their giving and that sounded great. But as he went on, he gave the impression that it was okay if they didn't want to give, because they had families and jobs and everything he doesn't have himself. It was as though he was negating the message, something he should be believing in. He missed the idea that you can be poor and struggling but still give back. So he was easing the blow, like making a cushion. But I don't think the call is cushiony. It's very vivid. I think we have a responsibility to learn what the call is and where I am personally with it. Because I think that's where stewardship really starts: "Where is my relationship with God?" Not what I'm doing in this church or giving to it, but where am I with God? Where is my heart? How am I giving? Not how much but how?

If you ask Marge, conversion occurs in steps. Only recently had she come to the conviction that, indeed, *everything*, including money, is a gift from God. Just because her husband earned it doesn't mean money isn't a gift. "I just had to come to grips with this whole thing," she admits. "Everything means everything."

How is sacrificial giving distinguished from stewardship? Or are they synonymous? Lou and Howie turned to the concept of "first fruits:" charitable giving comes ahead of all other bills to be paid (the Scholtzes recommend 5 percent of one's income to the church, 1 percent to the Bishops' Appeal, and 4 percent for other charities). This decision constitutes sacrificial giving, a practice that in turn opens the door to stewardship in its more inclusive sense, that is, giving also of one's time and talent. Marge paid less attention to this distinction:

> I think it's a matter of semantics. To be good stewards, we should be giving sacrificially. We're called from the moment we are baptized to be stewards and to be disciples. Good stewards are followers of Jesus Christ. Living it out is something else, but that is what we are forced to do. Of course, I'm not perfect, but my goal is to work toward that. I get back to the *how* of giving: I could be giving ten million dollars and giving with the wrong attitude or the wrong motives and it wouldn't matter. You know, the church would be richer but Margie would be poorer! All that is a lot different from giving out of some sense of obligation, which is what I did to the church for years.

Ginny also saw stewardship as going beyond sacrificial giving:

> It includes your time and your talent, recognizing you have those
> talents of yours to give. Don't say you lack talent. Everybody has
> something, trust me, something you're good at, that you'd be
> happy contributing. In giving our time and talent, you begin to get
> involved in the community called church. Then giving is not such
> a wrenching thing because you want to contribute toward that
> community. It almost flows after that. Once you let people feel they
> are part of the community—that will make the treasure come.

Witnessing to fellow parishioners about their own conversion experiences, both couples agreed, is vital to get others in the parish thinking about their own lives. But they all made reference to the central role
of prayer, "room for the Spirit to move in people's lives," as Marge put
it. Too much attention to figuring out different ways of getting the message across "can leave no room for the Spirit there."

Isn't it the case that, if we give generously, we know that God will
take care of us? Ginny answered:

> I think when I was growing up and learning religion, that was sort
> of implied. I think a lot of people will walk around with that in the
> back of their minds, people my age. Converting to stewardship
> enabled me to free myself from that, and it is a freedom to say, "I'm
> giving without conditions." Because you know what happens?
> When I give, I get anyway. But I'm not giving to get; it just hap-
> pens. And I'm not necessarily getting material things. In fact, you
> don't get material things. I'm getting a lot more than that.

The importance of lay witnessing is essential to deepening any
stewardship program. And even more importantly, those who work in
stewardship speak from the vantage point of their own conversion,
inspiring others to serve by sharing private and yet all too familiar
struggles.

Volunteers and Ministry:
Fostering the Growth of Time and Talent

St. Gerard's has abandoned the use of the term "volunteer" in favor
of the word "minister." Volunteer implies, in some people's minds, that
anybody can do any of the ministries offered in the stewardship program. This, it is felt, contradicts what St. Paul wrote in his First Letter
to the Corinthians (12:4-7 NRSV):

> Now there are varieties of gifts, but the same Spirit; and there are
> varieties of services, but the same Lord; there are different forms of
> service but the same Lord; and there are varieties of activities, but
> it is the same God who activates all of them in everyone. To each is
> given the manifestation of the Spirit for the common good.

Therefore the parish finds it helpful to talk about an annual recommit-
ment to ministries of service in the parish, and beyond to the community at large, using scriptural inspiration to encourage members to offer
their time and talent.

As one of the pastors pointed out, "We help people see that all
ministries listed are equally ways of doing stewardship. *All* the gifts
people have are needed. No one ministry, including the liturgical ones,
is more important than the others." Furthermore, ministries of service
not related to the church are given high esteem: volunteer firemen and
women; emergency medical technicians; Red Cross lifeguards; Candy-
stripers at local hospitals. Each way of serving is recommended publicly in the parish as a way of practicing stewardship.

In a letter to parishioners in April 1999, the two pastors reminded
parishioners:

> God has *plans* for your Christ-light to shine in the life and mission
> of our Parish church community and beyond. As priests called to
> serve as co-pastors, we believe God has planted in *each* of you spe-
> cific gifts and talents beneficial to St. Gerard Majella parishioners.
> And whether your gift is in the area of worship, or sharing the
> teachings of Jesus, or outreach services, or community building,
> there are persons *waiting* to welcome your gift of time and talent.

The remainder of their letter invited parishioners to the annual Ministry
Fair. Witness speakers would describe "the joy they received in sharing
their time and talent with others." The fair would be informational only,
encouraging parishioners to talk with ministry leaders and members
about what they might expect. The following two weeks would feature
invitations to respond by choosing "a ministry that best suits your
gifts." A Wednesday night in June was designated as Ministry Information Night for those desiring to explore a new ministry opportunity.

The above quote is from a four-page flyer that described the array
of ministries supported by the parish. The areas of service, each with a
brief description, includes entries that would sound familiar in any
parish: baptism sponsors, Pre-Cana program for engaged couples,

Christian Formation catechists, King's Kids for three- to six-year-olds, a Liturgy of the Word with children at the 9 A.M. Sunday Mass. At the latter, six- to nine-year-olds are sent forth to hear the Scripture readings in language they can better understand. They then rejoin their families at the Eucharist during the presentation of the gifts.

I was struck, too, by the Ministry of Consolation, which offers assistance to those who are seriously ill or who have suffered the loss of a loved one. Members of this ministry visit the sick and assist them. They also can provide help with the details of the funeral Mass and burial services. There is also the St. Gerard Majella Guild, which ministers to couples who want to have a child, those who have difficult pregnancies, and those who await their child's birth. The Guild also supports novenas to St. Gerard Majella each October.

No parishioner at St. Gerard need be uncertain about what his or her gifts for ministry may be, as may be seen in the next section.

Women at the Center

In Marie, the parish gifts coordinator, St. Gerard's is blessed with a person who has dedicated her life to pastoral ministry. Foremost among her responsibilities is spiritual gift discernment for parishioners uncertain about where their talents may lie. Marie helps them by explaining and administering the Spiritual Gift Assessment of 153 items called "Giftrak," developed by Church Growth Institute of Forest, Virginia. Upon completion of the assessment, Marie discusses with each parishioner the various parish ministries that would seem to suit his or her unique inclinations and talents. She then mails a letter of invitation to serve in a particular ministry or ministries. Marie's assistance is strengthened by telephone follow-up ministers, who make calls to those receiving letters. As others told me, among Marie's gifts is a vision of faith that came through in her interview. It is easy to understand the high regard she enjoys in her parish:

> In the season of Advent that is coming up, most people light Advent wreaths. Well, at home we light one big candle that we call the Mary candle. We say, "We wait and expect like she did." I always told my family, "We're *Ave* people: we're available, we're vulnerable, and we expect from God. This is what *Ave Maria* means." Mary is definitely our model of faith, someone very fragile and

gentle, yes, because she is female. A gentle creation, but powerful, too. Something fragile can be so strong if it's focused on God.

Marie brings Holy Communion to hospital patients, but her pastoral ministry is often conducted over the phone:

> People will call and say, "My husband just went into the hospital and I need to talk to a priest. I want him to pray with me." So I say, "Well, neither of the Fathers is available right now, but the Lord says, 'Whenever two or more are gathered, there I am in the middle.' How about it? I think maybe the Lord would like to lift you up in prayer. So many people right now are praying for your husband; it's you who need some peace. You want to pray?" Well, there's a pause, but every time the response has been, "Thank you, okay." Father Bill once said, "You know, you do a lot of pastoral work here." Well, does the Lord say we are priestly people or does he not? I simply believe what he says. My boss is Jesus Christ, and before I worked for the priests here, I worked for Him. That's what I love. I want to be with the people. I'm only here fourteen months and I love it. I understand a lot more. But the wisdom that can only come from God goes with you wherever you are. No one taught me that. It's the Lord who taught me.

Marie has also taken an active part in a prayer team begun at St. Gerard's, with members who agree to pray fifteen minutes a day. "We act as intercessors for this parish, that God's will be done in this community, within every ministry, and within the lives of our pastors. Trusting and believing." Team meetings, besides prayer, include songs, Scripture reading, and members sharing concerns.

Ready with Answers:
Responding to Parishioners' Misgivings and Objections

Distinctive of St. Gerard's is the forthright way in which the co-pastors responded to misgivings and objections to the treasure dimension of stewardship. Not all parishioners saw stewardship as favorably as Rosemary, Penny, Marie, or the witnessing couples. Parishioner resistance was at times strong and vocal, not unusual in a parish beginning stewardship. The co-pastors decided to meet this resistance head on.

Father Heller's overall statement to the parish is an excellent example of how to bring forward the theology of stewardship—extending it to key issues (in parentheses):

> Resistance to the stewardship of our material goods, including the stewardship of our money, is often rooted in the failure of a focused and faith-filled acceptance of one's life as gifted, rooted and lived out in the baptismal mystery of the Trinity *(the issue here is God's abundant and life-sustaining self-gift),* a life modeled on the paschal mystery of Christ's life, death, and resurrection *(the issue here is a conversion, becoming a servant of God's Word on every level),* which is exacted and lived out in a faith community context *(the issue is our ecclesial nature at work, home, school, play and at rest)* for the life of the world *(the issues here are economic distribution and social justice).*

Not content to express stewardship solely in theological terms, Father Heller wrote a hard-hitting response to what he and Father Hanson were hearing from parishioners concerning sacrificial giving. I reproduce it in full for two reasons: First, virtually any parish beginning stewardship can expect the same reactions; and secondly, because Father Heller's answers continue to evoke the theology of stewardship, resisting any temptation to talk about "parish needs" or "your obligation to support your parish." This document, I believe, could readily serve as a model for any parish attempting to meet parishioners' misgivings.

Ten Questions and Statements and Some Answers
Regarding Sacrificial Giving [3]

1. "No one is going to force this stewardship stuff down my throat and tell me what to give."

   Response: No one is *trying* to tell you *what* to give. Sacrificial Giving is an invitation to put God first in all that we have and do, specifically in the uses of our time, talent, and treasure. *How* we use the gifts God has given us is our response, which can range from thoughtlessness to thankfulness.

---

[3] Letter by Father Christopher Heller on sacrificial giving. Reprinted with permission.

2. "I don't like using envelopes—it's a matter of principle for me. And any-way, it's a private matter between me and God."

   Response: Even more important than providing a record of weekly and annual giving, using an envelope every week means that I be-lieve in my parish enough to make a commitment to supporting it. Also, wrapping my gift in an envelope makes a deliberate and con-scious statement: this envelope contains my gift to continue God's work in our parish this week.

3. "I just give spontaneously, whatever I have in my pocket."

   Response: Planned giving each week—whatever the specific amount it is—helps to put and keep God first, rather than giving to God's work whatever I have left over. And since my sacrificial gift goes for the work of the church and the care of the poor in our parish, my planned gift allows the pastor and pastoral staff to plan how best to help those in need.

4. "I've never heard of this Sacrificial Giving stuff in the Roman Catholic Church, and I've been a Catholic all my life. It sounds strange to me."

   Response: That's understandable, given the fact that lots of Roman Catholic fund-raising has been done through bake sales, carnivals, Bingo games and the like. To be accurate, the idea of giving a *por-tion* of all that I have—my time, my talent, and my treasure—is over five thousand years old. It occurs in both the Hebrew Scrip-tures of the Old Testament as well as the Christian Scriptures of the New Testament.

5. "I'm very angry that the priest is talking about money. I came to church to hear about the Gospel, and talk about money is out of place."

   Response: Each week in the Profession of Faith, we renew our promise to follow the words and actions of Jesus, God's Chosen One. In over half of his parables, Jesus talked about money and material possessions and how we use them in our daily lives. Be-cause the use of money and other physical resources was a concern of Jesus, it has to be a concern of ours so that we can hear the entire message that Jesus came to bring us.

6. "I come to church to escape the problems of daily life, not to be reminded of my responsibility to respond to others' needs."

   Response: To be sure, one reason why we come to church is to receive God's consolation and to deepen our relationship with our God. But being a member of this church also includes becoming more sensitive to other community members and my relationships with them. Coming to church is more about our being strengthened to deal with life's daily problems rather than to escape them. God did not spare Jesus from suffering and death, but helped Jesus to continue to grow *through and in spite of the suffering he endured.*

7. "All the church is concerned about is money."

Response: Yes, it's a shock the first time we hear that the money in our pockets is not our money, but that it's been entrusted to us. In addition to being consumers, we are *stewards* and are accountable to God for how we use our time, talent, and material possessions. All three of these dimensions are important. In fact, for years other Christian churches have been calling their members to sacrifice in these three areas by contributing one of their talents one hour a week and contributing weekly to the support of the parish.

8. "If time and talent are so important, why did we hear about treasure first? It makes me feel that time and talent are not as important as money."

Response: Actually, the parish invites people from the pulpit and in the bulletin *all year round* for people to donate their time and talent: readers, catechists, ushers, visitors to homebound and nursing home patients, communion ministers, and so on. While you may not have heard these invitations described as examples of time and talent, each and all of them involve a personal sacrifice, and a personal commitment to them benefits our neighbors and strengthens our relationship with God.

9. "I've always felt that the church should spend more time talking about spiritual things, not things of this world."

Response: People of every age have tried to suggest that there are two worlds, the world of the spirit and the world of earthly things. The Jesuit poet Gerard Manley Hopkins, in accord with the Bible's creation story, wrote that "the world is charged with the grandeur of God." The fact that God only made one world: these two kinds of concerns are interwoven with each other, and I can't separate them. There is a spiritual dimension to time, talent, and treasure, just as there is a practical dimension to living a whole and spiritual life. In fact, it involves a *holy* use of money for God's purposes.

10. "I'm angry when I hear these Sacrificial Giving presentations."

Response: It's not unusual to be disturbed when I hear something new and challenging. Being able to pinpoint *what* makes you angry can be helpful. To be specific:

—you've received an invitation to think differently about the pattern and quality of your giving, one that asks for a response.

—you've already made up your mind not to accept the invitation to examine your giving patterns on any level.

—you've realized that you *could* be more generous, but that the change will be hard because it will mean sacrifice.

—you've believed that the gifts of time, talent, and material possessions are private matters between you and God even though you know that it's *people* who benefit when other people are generous.

—you're convinced that the parish is sitting on lots of money, and you aren't interested in looking at your own desire to give.

—you know how difficult it is to make a commitment, and that the pastor has no right to ask this commitment of you.

—you still believe that you go to your parish church to *receive* and not primarily to give.

—you've been able to pick and choose how and when you would be involved in the parish, and now you're being asked to look at your whole pattern of involvement, and that's uncomfortable.

—you feel that you should be accountable to no one other than God.

—you are not comfortable when things change, and changes that have to do with the church are even more difficult.

Whatever annoys or angers you about this invitation to Sacrificial Giving for members of the Catholic Church probably is part of a *picture* you have in your mind about giving to God and God's work. And because the picture is connected to *attitudes* that are lived out in *daily behavior,* it can be upsetting for someone to paint a new picture of new possibilities and options. In all these questions, emotions, and issues, it is still possible that God may be asking you to take a step toward this new way of practicing your Catholic Christian faith. Of course, how you respond to God's invitation through the Church is your choice. It's by examining your heart that you will be able to understand how generously your return to God will be.

(Signed)
Father Chris Heller

In Retrospect

"Nowhere to go but up" aptly defines what the co-pastors initially faced: a parish in woeful shape. By their own admission, their first three years were spent floundering in financial desperation. But St. Gerard's was also situated in one of the nation's largest metropolitan complexes, which meant that resources were at hand to which they could turn. In this case, Monsignor John Bracken of the neighboring Brooklyn Diocese, a board member of the National Catholic Stewardship Council, brought them into contact with sacrificial giving and stewardship. Diocesan-level resources, as other parishes in this book remind us, often serve to introduce and support stewardship. This support did not exempt the pastors, as their vivid and often humorous accounts tell us, from going through a personal conversion process essential to effective pastoral stewardship.

Moreover, the pastors shared their struggles with the parishioners, an experience that helped them confront directly any misgivings about stewardship broached by disgruntled parishioners. Their open attitudes also engendered feelings of mutual respect—priests, parishioners and parish staff—all on the "side" of making stewardship work at St. Gerard Majella Parish.

Especially memorable were the intense reflections by Fathers Heller and Hanson. Both pastors wanted to move beyond "parish needs" and "an obligation to support the parish." Sacrificial giving was to be established as primary, interwoven with a theology of stewardship. Using envelopes weekly as opposed to keeping "God first" in a sacrificial context was insufficient. "Whatever I have left over" simply wouldn't be adequate anymore, period. The theology of stewardship made it imperative to bypass bake sales, carnivals, whatever "added up" in terms of very familiar sales. Having an *entire* message was primary.

Close at hand was another resource: couples such as Howie and Marge, and Lou and Ginny, who were already imbued with stewardship ideals when Fathers Hanson and Heller arrived on the scene. They had experienced, and helped to develop, a strong core community at St. Gerard's that reinforced and supported the stewardship initiatives of the two pastors in the face of considerable parishioner resistance. Both couples helped, by virtue of their involvement in diocesan-wide stewardship efforts (including their heartfelt witnessing in other parishes), to establish St. Gerard's as a parish that took stewardship seriously. Growth in the time and talent dimension of stewardship was immeasurably aided by "core parishioners" like Rosemary and Penny.

St. Gerard's has also been blessed with extraordinary parish staff members, as we have seen. To the pastors'credit, they recognized early on the talents and deep spirituality of women in the parish. The pastors responded by giving full scope for the exercise of gifts they valued. These women were encouraged to develop major roles in pastoral care. Marie's gifts of spiritual discernment, her willingness to help people find their "true gifts," have proved a great blessing to time and talent recruitment within the parish (every parish should have a Marie!).

Marie helped to introduce Ministry Information Night to the parish, during which new parishioners were invited to learn about ways in which they might serve. Their contributions have freed the co-pastors for more active contact with parishioners rather than being confined to their desks for a good part of each day.

Also commendable is the extension of the stewardship umbrella to all service occupations represented in the parish. Firefighters and medical technicians are among those referred to as practicing stewardship of their talents. All this furthers the process of making stewardship a guiding paradigm for the parish.

St. Gerard's once again underlines the uphill struggle that awaits any parish that takes a stewardship approach seriously, that is, the parish decision to take stewardship way beyond a ritual invocation during the fall pledge campaign. When this effort begins to bear fruit, as it has here, it carries truly transformative potential for any Catholic parish.

PART III

Advanced Stewardship

Chapter 6

We Measure the Depth of Our Faith by the Breadth of Our Outreach to Those in Need

CHURCH OF ST. JOHN THE BAPTIST
COVINGTON, WASHINGTON

The late archbishop of Seattle, Most Rev. Raymond G. Hunthausen, achieved national recognition for his prophetic stands against nuclear-armed submarines, not hesitating to demonstrate publicly and risk arrest in attempting to arouse the consciences of Seattle Catholics about the deadly industries in their community. Less widely known was his support for innovation in Seattle parishes. As greater Seattle pushed southward, planning took shape for a new parish in the small city of Kent, out of which grew Covington, the parish's present community. A group of forward-looking lay archdiocesan advisers suggested that the new parish be based on stewardship. The archbishop approved. In 1990 a small group of families gathered in a public school hall to form the new parish. It was different from the start. I interviewed the pastor of St. John the Baptist Parish, Fr. Jack Walmesley, when I visited in June 1996. He began:

> We were in a public school for five years. Stewardship was simply easier to do there. The only people who came were there because they wanted to. Period. They had to sit on hard metal chairs and look around at all the chalkboard and announcements and kids' drawings. We had a wonderful liturgy but not a very nice space. But it meant that we were a very intentional parish. And as an intentional way of life, stewardship had more resonance than it might in a more established parish.

Stewardship had gained a foothold in the parish in early 1992, when fund-raising for a future church became a central issue. Pastor and parishioners interviewed several firms that did a more traditional form of fund-raising. In the process they talked with Seattle consultant Jim Burns, a man imbued with the ideals of stewardship. Father Walmesley continued:

> He came out with a whole different approach that included the spirituality of stewardship—time, talent, plus the money. So after wrestling with parish leadership for several months, we made the decision that it was worth it. To take a risk. We would start the parish off on this basis [integrating capital fund raising with stewardship] rather than switching to stewardship later. So we hired Jim to do a campaign, but it wasn't just money. We asked people (and we still do) to sign up for time and for talent and for treasure.

By the time of my visit in 1996, the parish had grown to over six hundred households and was enjoying a new parish facility completed six months previously.

What is the background of your parishioners?

> Very technology-oriented. We have working-class people, but we also have a huge number of engineers. Lots work for Boeing of course. Median income in our parish is around $42,000. Good number of teachers, too.

I was impressed by how articulate the members of your Parish Council were the other night.

> Exactly. From my perspective of twenty-two years as a priest, it's the most talented parish, skillwise or leadershipwise [that] I've ever been in. I've been in parishes where you couldn't get anyone to lead. Just followers and doers. Leaders are just here in abundance. It really makes a difference in implementing a program because you can give it to them and they run with it. And they report back. This is a pattern they learn at work.

Stewardship: The Program

I have no hesitation in quoting directly and at some length from the parish's attractive and professional quality brochure "Stewardship

Program." This 1992 statement was the early outcome of the parish community's striving to articulate what stewardship means and the commitments it requires. Its formulations could serve as a model for any church, regardless of denomination. A parish mission statement opens the brochure:

> We, the Catholic faith community of St. John the Baptist, declare this to be our identity and our mission:
>
> *We value our Catholic heritage.* We try to live out those values in parish and individual lives.
>
> *We value community* and believe that diversity and participation can only strengthen community. We make our parish a place of welcome, a safe haven for all who wish to belong.
>
> *We value the life of the Spirit.* We strive to deepen our spiritual lives and to be open to the sign of the Holy Spirit working in the world.
>
> *We value service.* We measure the depth of our faith by the breadth of our outreach to those in need.
>
> *We value worship.* At the core of our identity as a parish lies our experience with liturgy and the Sacraments which bring us into communion with each other and with our Lord.
>
> *We value each other.* We listen to each other; we share with each other. Our goal is to be a community that lives the values of St. John the Baptist: prayer, service, love, and justice.

The brochure continues, with illustrative photos, to underline the primary parish goals of worshiping together, conducting educational programs, and rendering service to one another and to those in need. Stewardship is clearly stated as an enabling program in relation to these goals:

> Your giving of *Time, Talent, and Money* enriches the quality of our worship together. Your giving of *Time, Talent, and Money* helps us provide quality and effective education programs for our children and ourselves.

There follows an exceptionally well-crafted stewardship statement:

> Stewardship flows out of an understanding and acknowledgment that everything we are and have is a Gift from God. When we give

a portion of our time, talent, and money to our parish and to the wider community, we are Giving Witness to our commitment to this reality and we express our gratitude to God for what we have been given.

Giving is subsequently elaborated in three dimensions. Each dimension manifests the intent that the parish strives for in member commitment:

> *Our Giving is Planned:* The decision to give is just that—a decision. It requires *Planning,* prayer and thought, so that it is not a spur of the moment decision. Giving is integrated with our other decisions as part of a careful, intentional response to God's generosity.
>
> *Our Giving is Sacrificial:* In a world full of human needs, the word *Sacrifice* in our faith tradition means that we give up something in order to make something good possible. Every parent who sacrifices something for their children understands this. At *St. John the Baptist* we call each other to give up something in order to fulfill our dreams of serving one another and all of God's people.
>
> *Our Giving is Proportionate:* Part of our planning ensures that we give in *Proportion* to what we have been given. Some people use the Biblical concept of the tithe, a tenth, as a guide to giving of money, but in any case, the gifts of time, talent, and money are in proportion with what we have been given. Our gifts of money do not substitute for gifts of time and talent. Neither do time and talent substitute for giving financial resources. All our gifts, as St. Paul states, are given for the sake of the community. God's gifts are given in order to give life to others.

The meaning of "gifts of time and talent" is not left to parishioners' imaginations. An entire page of the brochure speaks to this issue, beginning with a firm expectation of what membership in this worship community involves: Each member is asked to consider giving ten or more hours per month of their time and talent to meet parish, community, and family needs. Parishioners are asked to "review and check the areas (listed below) you are presently working in or are interested in exploring for your commitment hours. . . ." Forty-five ministries are listed for parishioners to choose an activity that interests them. Following the ministry list is the statement: "A parish volunteer will visit your home to answer any questions you have and to receive your Covenant Form." The brochure is equally clear in explaining the importance of financial support for stewardship, taking the parishioner directly, frankly, and specifically into the stewardship of monetary giving:

> Along with Time and Talent each parish member or family is asked to give a planned, proportionate and sacrificial amount of their annual income to the parish and to set aside an equal amount for other community needs. Specifically, you are asked to consider giving two hours of your weekly wages to the Parish per week and set aside in reserve an equal amount for needs in the wider community.

A chart follows, suggesting dollar guidelines for giving, beginning with an "Annual Income" column followed by "Approximate Hourly Wage," "Giving 1 to 2 Hours' Wages per Week," and a resulting "Monthly Gift to Parish."

Father Walmesley and a delegation from the parish had visited St. Francis of Assisi Parish in Wichita, Kansas. Inspired by the methods that St. Francis had developed to encourage families to give of their treasure, Father Walmesley created a ministry sign-up form that asks parish members to list family members, including head of household, spouse, and the number of children in grades one through six. The parish then provides the family with tithing envelopes, including special ones for the children. He explains, "We try to get them to recognize some stewardship of their allowances."

Lastly, the Covenant Commitment completes the invitation to stewardship in this community:

> I/We pledge to live out as best I/we can the *Values* of St. John the Baptist Parish by giving a planned portion of my *Time, Talent and Money* to the parish and the wider community. *Lord, give me/us the gift of faith and grace to do this.*
>
> I will give the following _____ hours of my Time and Talent per month in gratitude to God for what I have been given and to live out the Parish Mission of St. John the Baptist. *Lord, give me/us the gift of wisdom to do this.*
>
> I/We intend to use the Sunday Offertory Envelope to give an average of $_____ per week in gratitude to God for what I/we have been given to live out the Parish Mission of St. John the Baptist. *Lord, give me/us the gift of courage to do this.*

In no way are stewardship ideals expressed in lofty or "fuzzy" terms, leaving interpretation up to each parishioner or parish household.

Intent is the key here: inviting church members to think deliberately about suggested norms of giving time, talent, and money. To be a member, then, entails a serious commitment and, as all the literature on growing churches suggests, such churches attract people precisely because they "cost" and, simultaneously, because those costs underlie visible, meaningful, and attractive ministries to both the church and the wider community.

Reflecting on the Program

Father Walmesley is understandably pleased that approximately 85 percent of the members sign the covenant. And while he is content to use the archdiocesan plan of asking Catholics to "take a step up" each year in monetary giving, he would like to go beyond that:

> We're not afraid to use the word "tithe," and I find people quite responsive to it. It's like, Okay, we're not asking for a full ten percent right off the bat, but we'd like you to move toward it—that's where we tie into the archdiocesan approach. Now we have an expanded notion of stewardship that comes in here as far as time and talent go. On our ministry form, we acknowledge that people are doing stewardship of their time outside of church: They're coaching Little League or perhaps they're leaning over the fence talking to a neighbor who's going through a divorce. We try to get people to develop a sense that they are doing far more than they give themselves credit for. None of this "If you're not around the parish, you're not giving of time and talent." Stewardship of time is sharing talents in the larger community, too. Even just being at work, you may be listening to someone going through a hard time. We often preach on this, just saying recognize what you're already doing.

Father Walmesley suspects that as the parish grows, the percentage of parishioners who pledge to give will go down:

> Before I was here, I was personnel director for the priests of the archdiocese. I visited every parish in the archdiocese. I could see a correlation: If you had a parish of five hundred households, you could probably count on four hundred giving. Now you'd think that when you got to one thousand households you'd get eight hundred giving. Well, you don't. You might get six hundred out of

a thousand. We're trying very hard here not to let people get away with that and to challenge them with something.

Evidence that the challenge is successful lies in the fact that 85 percent of households that "make a commitment to giving something financially" commit also to giving of time and talent in some form. Each "giving unit" gets a quarterly statement of their giving record.

> I sign all these statements. They indicate that you committed to such-and-such, year to date. You've done this and we thank you for your commitment. And on about 90 percent of them, I write a little personal note. So I am aware of just where they are and who's maintaining and who isn't.

In cases of those falling behind, Father Walmesley either writes a note or, "if the situation looks quite dramatic," may phone them:

> "I noted that you dropped off. Is there some way we can help you?" This is an emphasis we have here: we are available to help you. In fact, we started a seed fund, euphemistically called "The Mormon Fund." Out of this fund we help parishioners financially who have suffered a serious setback. One of the few "extra" fund-raisers we do is an auction. This year we took in about $15,000. Almost all of it went into the fund to help parishioners. And this is separate from what we give to St. Vincent de Paul. For example, the mother of a family here has leukemia. Her bill, beyond Medicare, is $1,000 per month. We pick up about $400 of that per month. This is part of stewardship, of course. So if people give substantially, we can enable people to count on their parish, not for everything, but for something.

> *So you have this auction as an "extra" fundraiser?*

> In view of stewardship, you can't be doing extra fund-raisers all over the place. This is the only one we're doing right now. We had quite a debate about it. Several had said, "We're on this steward-ship track, but now it seems we're taking a step back." So we decided to do a parish poll in which we simply asked, "If we have a fund-raising option, would it appear to you that we are taking a backward step in stewardship?" The great majority said they didn't think so, but all cautioned, if we get to ten of these [a year], we'd be fund-raising almost every month. And we've been very careful not to do that. In fact, the focus of the auction has not been

so much fund-raising, but rather as a community event. We had about four hundred people come to it this year.

The poll suggests to me you're comfortable with collective decision-making.

Yes. It's my personal style. It's also a sort of theology of the parish. Hopefully, the parishioners are going to be here a lot longer than I am. I'd like to see them develop a sense of ownership. That, I think, goes along with a spirit of stewardship. In any case, I think they know that decisions are pretty broad-based here, that I don't ram things through.

Your stance helps develop a sense of trust too.

Right. If we think of it as the stewardship of *my* parish versus the stewardship of *their* parish, we're all going to lose. What's really important is the sense people here have of co-responsibility and real authority. That more than 80 percent who are involved know that the parish relies on them. "It's pretty clear we're not going to make it, folks, if we're not involved." So they have a great sense of responsibility. They know their input is valued.

Some pastors, though, feel that finances are their personal territory.

Some years ago at a deanery meeting, the idea came up of the arch-diocese doing a regular audit of each parish, maybe each year, maybe every two years. High-level resistance: "No way!" I was kind of surprised. If they want to do that at our parish, fine, be-cause we actually have what amounts to an audit every month. One member of our finance committee goes through every single check expenditure asking what is this for, why is that here? What is this? This all goes back to whose money is this? The old theology emphasized this area as the pastor's alone, and a lot of priests still have that sense. I do feel responsible for the money in the parish, but I don't feel *personally* responsible. I feel that it's responsible enough to know that the finance committee really goes through that check register with a fine-toothed comb. But other pastors might sense a loss of power or control of finances doing it the way we do here.

Speaking of finances, a frequent question is, What do people get back from the giving they're asked to do?

You often hear, "Give that it might be given back to you." But not in the sense of money, you know, if you give $100, then you get $1,000 back. The mystery of Christianity is that in giving your life

away through your generosity, you receive a full life—I'm talking
about quality of life—a sense of purpose, direction, a sense, too, of
living out your commitment. The result is a sense of well-being,
of making a contribution. It all comes back to you this way as
opposed to a more selfish way of life.

I have wondered whether stewardship is really countercultural.

I start with a theme of the common culture we share. I think Christianity does fly in the face of so many values present in our society.
It's a theme I use quite often: There is a countercultural piece to
being a Christian. From a Catholic perspective, we try to be leaven
or salt; we're not a sect, after all. We're not into that kind of aliena-
tion. What we do say is that where so many cultural values around
us are afoot, stewardship is not afoot. We have to choose. My sense
is that, as Catholics, we don't address the differences between
Christianity and our culture as strongly as, say, the more funda-
mentalist churches would. I wouldn't want to set up a holy war
against our society, but nevertheless we are affected by the culture
we share.

1998–2000: Enacting a Master Plan for Growth

I returned for a visit in the fall of 1998 to find St. John the Baptist a
thriving parish of over seven hundred families. The median annual
income had risen to $87,500, and expanding parish facilities was on
everyone's mind. Father Walmesley set about exploring every avenue
of financing the new additions. In a letter to the archdiocesan Parish
Revolving Fund Board in October 1998, he pointed to the high growth
rate of the Covington community. The parish, he noted, "is weighted
towards younger families with children . . . the proposed expansion is
part of the original plan to provide additional space for basic parish
programs and activities when financial resources are available."
Urgently needed were classrooms, a social hall, and meeting spaces.
A three-year capital campaign was launched. In a letter to Father
Walmesley in July 1998, the archdiocesan director of Parish Financial
Services, Ed Williams, complimented St. John the Baptist Parish:

In short, your parish has been successful in implementing one of
the strongest Stewardship-based financial plans in the Archdiocese. The Tithing Rate for St. John the Baptist is higher than for

any of your neighboring parishes and substantially higher than most. In addition, your parish has strong participation in the Sacrificial Giving aspect of Stewardship as reflected by the 80+ percent of your households using envelopes vs. the archdiocesan average of less than 50 percent.

Williams underlined the importance of major gifts ($100,000 or over) to encourage strong parish total giving. Significantly, he remarked that "a campaign in your parish will require a great deal of education since it will be a new concept for many of your original parishioners. You should seriously consider a feasibility study before you commit to a drive."

St. John the Baptist Parish did take seriously the notion of "education" prior to launching the capital campaign. "A feasibility study" translated into seeking parish consensus, a practice deriving from earliest days when a few families gathered in a public school classroom. The way this process was carried out strikingly illustrates stewardship as collective, and in this case also creative, responsibility for the welfare of the parish.

Communication: Seeking Parish Consensus

In early 1997, 40 percent of parishioners responded to a written priority survey. Religious education and youth programs were the top two vote-getters out of seven priorities listed. Parish expansion was third, but a more specific "expanding facilities" fell to sixth place. As John Baumann, pastoral associate, remarked, "The connection between facilities and programs was lacking for many. We spent one year making the connection."

The "connecting" process that followed is remarkable. Several phases evolved, all with the purpose of soliciting parishioners' views as the basis of the planning effort. The following were instrumental in achieving a consensus.

1. Focus Groups

Members of the Stewardship Council invited parishioners to give their views of parish needs. They designated five Sundays, between February and June 1999, for parishioners to express their perspectives.

Each Sunday was dedicated to a specific age group: under 18; 18 to 29; 30 to 39; 40 to 55; 55 and over. Results of these listening sessions were summarized and distributed to parishioners as a list of priorities to be considered.

2. CIRCLE MASSES

Since the worship space at St. John the Baptist is completely open, that is, with no pews or fixed seats, flexible seating is easy to arrange. Holding a Circle Mass means that parishioners coming to weekend Masses seat themselves at tables with six to eight chairs. The pastor invites each person to introduce himself or herself to those at the table. In lieu of the sermon, each attendee discusses with others at the table whatever topic or issues, chosen from a page available to each person, that have occasioned this event. Each table then selects one person to record responses on a Group Response Sheet. In this case the page listed seven priorities identified in the focus group sessions. The pastor acted as facilitator for each session. The form on page 104 entitled "Circle Mass Feedback" reproduces the priorities sheet. Father Walmesley encouraged those at each table to share their comments on the priorities. Each attendee was then to make his or her ranking of the listed priorities. Results of the ranking process yielded the following top priorities: (1) expanding educational enrichment opportunities; (2) expanding ministry to youth; (3) building additional facilities (classrooms, meeting space, a social hall).

Next, a Building Expansion Committee composed of parishioners representing various areas of parish life—facilities, education, youth— was formed. The committee's charge was to produce preliminary plans for building expansion based on current and future needs of the parish. The various desiderata compiled in focus groups and Circle Masses were taken into account. Subsequently an architect was brought in to help visualize what the proposed expansion would look like, including budget estimates for the components of the preliminary drawings.

3. OPINION SURVEY

Once again parish members were asked for input regarding the findings of the Building Expansion Committee. Two sessions were held. The first consisted of parishioners randomly chosen according to

Circle Mass Feedback
Determining Parish Priorities
For 1998

The following priorities were identified through our parish FOCUS GROUPS, the survey questions presented by Father Jack during Mass in April, and discussion by the parish leadership. The parish leadership (Ministerial and Stewardship Councils along with all commissions) needs your input in determining where we should allocate our resources during the coming year.

Please rank the following parish priorities 1 through 7, with 1 representing the top priority in your opinion.

_____ Expand schedule of parish social activities (i.e., dances, family movie nights, pot luck gatherings)

_____ Expand the idea and understanding of what it means to be disciples in a Stewardship Parish (i.e., an all parish retreat/mission, individual retreats focusing specifically on stewardship)

_____ Give 10% of parish income to the poor inside and outside the parish (i.e., increasing contributions to Catholic Community Services, St. Vincent de Paul and Parish Social Action Fund)

_____ Provide more opportunities for spiritual enrichment (i.e., parish led by experienced retreat masters, resources for home based retreats, individual spiritual direction)

_____ Expand parish facilities (i.e., additional classrooms, meeting space, social hall)

_____ Expand ministry to youth (i.e., fund a full-time youth ministry coordinator)

_____ Expand educational enrichment opportunities for adults and children (i.e., bible study programs, develop small faith sharing groups, guest lecture series and workshops)

Please share any additional comments/ideas below:

_____

_____

_____

how long they had been in the parish and whether they were active or simply on the fringe of parish life. All parishioners were invited to the second session, which was held after every Mass in late February and early March 1999. As the parish's final Needs Assessment Report explained:

> These sessions included an overview of the history of this project, an opportunity for questions to be posed; presentation by parishioners on the need for additional facilities; presentation of plans and costs; group and individual prayer and reflection time; answers to questions posed at the beginning of the session; a final question and answer period; and the opportunity to complete an opinion survey.

4. FINAL REVIEW AND GO-AHEAD

The results of these last surveys led to a decision by the Ministerial Council (the parish governing body) to present to the parish their assessment of current and future space needs along with recommendations. This presentation took place during all the Masses on a weekend in May 1999. Parishioners were asked to respond: Was now the time to proceed with building expansion? The results were strongly positive. In June the Ministerial Council gave the green light to pursue construction of both classrooms and a parish hall.

It would be hard to find a better example of open communication and solicitation of views leading to a sense of ownership by parishioners. Nothing was in any sense foisted upon them by parish leadership. From the outset, parishioners were invited to take part in the reflective and decision-making processes leading to construction of new facilities. The outcome would truly be theirs. One is reminded of a passage from the bishops' letter on stewardship:

> Parishes, too, must be, or become, true communities of faith within which [the] Christian life is learned and practiced . . . pastors and parish staff must be open, consultative, collegial, and accountable in the conduct of affairs. And parishioners must accept responsibility for their parishes and contribute generously—both money and personal service—to their programs and projects.[1]

[1] National Conference of Catholic Bishops, *Stewardship: A Disciple's Response* (Washington: United States Catholic Conference, 1992) 34.

The Capital Campaign

The title on the capital campaign brochure reads, "Stewardship: Embracing Life as God Intends." The parish mission statement occupies the first page. A letter from Father Walmesley follows, invoking the centrality of stewardship:

> In a spirit of Stewardship, financial prudence, and Christian simplicity we have managed for these nine years; however, based on parishioner input and reflection by your parish leadership, the appropriate time has arrived to address our facility needs. In this brochure you will see both the reason for expansion and the proposal to meet those needs. . . . A proclamation in our parish Mission Statement says, "We measure the depth of our faith by the breadth of our outreach to those in need." In order to respond to our Mission Statement and to assist other Catholic communities in great need, our parish will increase our outreach fund from our Sunday offering by one percent of all capital funds raised. This act of "Stewardship" on our part will help us respond to the words of Pope John Paul that the American Catholic Church be particularly aware of those in need.

After presenting detailed plans of the building expansion budget as well as ways to give—cash, checks, stocks, bonds, real estate, for example—the brochure concludes with a "St. John the Baptist Stewardship Prayer" that begins:

> Loving God, we are grateful for the abundant gifts you have given the community of St. John the Baptist. We hear your call to be good stewards of your gifts of time, talent, and treasure. We hear your call to share our talents to build a community worthy of your love. We thank You for the opportunity to share with all those whose lives we touch on our faith journey.

At no point, then, does this parish lose track of the stewardship theme, finding appropriate ways to insert its meaning into virtually every parish endeavor.

The campaign has indeed achieved success. Begun in January 1999, by April 569 out of the parish total of 714 households had been contacted. Father Walmesley led a parish team to visit potential major givers ($10,000 on up), from which thirty-nine givers pledged a total of $536,650 for an average pledge of $13,670. Out of the 530 remaining households contacted by parish teams, 392 pledged $794,120 for an average pledge of $2,026.

More remarkable, perhaps, is that ordinary financial giving seems to have suffered little from the impact of the capital campaign. Giving for 2000 saw 597 families out of 779 registered pledge an average annual amount of $1,183. This represents a 9.1 percent increase in giving over 1999. The stewardship of treasure, then, continues to enjoy a healthy status at St. John the Baptist.

Stewardship as Gift of Time and Talent

While the volunteer spirit has always been strong at St. John the Baptist, its character is perhaps best captured in the orientation of new members. Following every weekend liturgy, at a highly visible welcome table in the narthex, volunteers answer questions and assist those interested in completing a Request to Register form. Upon completing the form, prospective members are given information about the next Welcome Gathering, at which actual registration takes place.

The Welcome Gathering is a significant event in the parish, occurring about every six weeks, alternating Friday nights and Saturday mornings. Every attending individual or family that does not have a Bible is given one. Of central importance is the format of faith sharing. Parish members designated as facilitators lead those present in sharing significant points in their faith journeys. Inquirers present are asked what they have come to seek, along with what gifts or talents they hope to share. Facilitators review information about the parish, and a membership packet is given to each inquirer. Registration forms are completed and pictures are taken.

The pictures taken are posted in the narthex for at least three months, along with information about each new family or individual. Members of the Ministry Assist Team contact new parishioners within two weeks: Is there any ministry they wish to explore or be put in touch with right away? Signing people up is not an immediate priority. "Space" is accorded each new member to explore if he or she is uncertain about where to volunteer. Those newcomers wishing to participate in a given ministry are put in touch with the coordinator of that ministry (new members are also invited, about a month after the Welcome Gathering, to pledge financially to the parish).

Four times a year "Pizza with the Pastor" takes place. Those who have registered two to five months previously are invited to join the pastor and pastoral staff for an informal meal and learn more about the parish. Those attending are encouraged to ask questions on any subject. During weekend Masses these new members are invited to come forward for a blessing and introduction to the parish community.

Not surprisingly, the parish rarely lacks for volunteers in any area of need. In recent years the Stewardship Council has provided for each interested parishioner a Ministry Resource Book. The 1998 booklet lists approximately forty-five ministries, opening with the three central "councils": Ministerial (often called the "parish council" or "pastoral council" in other parishes); Financial, and Stewardship. The Stewardship Council, in turn, supports a Community Life Committee that gives rise to over a dozen subcommittee ministries ranging from nursery and newsletter to funeral receptions, donuts and coffee, and social events.

Four major commissions, each of which sponsors committees that seek volunteers, complete the structure of ministries: Facilities and Grounds; Religious Formation; Social Action; and Worship. The Resource Book, under each ministry, lists its purpose, the service it provides, its sponsor (pastor or pastoral associate), its meeting time and place, its recruiting period (including terms of service), and a time-commitment estimate (five hours a month). Most would be familiar to any parish: Legion of Mary, St. Vincent de Paul, religious education programs for various age groups. But a few are less familiar. Moms and Tots contains the description "Moms and children age five and under get together [weekly] in a casual atmosphere to share ideas, talk, and let children play and learn." Or an AIDS ministry described as: (1) providing support for those living with or affected with AIDS; (2) helping with fund raising for AIDS-related charities; (3) working with the Chicken Soup Brigade in providing delivery of weekly food to people living with or affected by AIDS; (4) providing AIDS education and awareness.

Willows, a grief support group, provides a "supportive environment in a small group for dealing with loss by death, divorce, or separation."

The Ministry Assist Team provides the following services: (1) matching skills/interests to parish functions; (2) identifying gift potential through self-awareness techniques; (3) supporting parishioners' pursuit of balance between family and parish commitments.

"Pursuit of balance" is a theme the parish has taken seriously in recent years and merits fuller description. Pastoral associate John Baumann's M.A. thesis for Seattle University's School of Theology and Ministry is entitled "Fostering Discernment in a Parish Community."

Given the large numbers of young families in the parish, it is no surprise that parents and children experience overcrowded schedules. "Ceaseless activities fills their lives," Baumann wrote. He believes that "many families caught in this lifestyle recognize its danger and attempt to move away from this frenetic, almost ceaseless activity." Rarely, however, do they consider eliminating one or more activities. Instead, "they attempt to create space through better control of time," which Baumann regards as a "futile attempt" that usually fails.

The primary role of parish staff members is to serve as a resource for the community. However, they find that they experience similar struggles with time management, particularly in relation to meetings and planning involving the various commissions, committees, and task groups. A great deal of time is consumed in securing more volunteers for the various parish organizations and ministries. "The emphasis became having everyone in the parish sign up for something . . . the primary focus shifted to the act of signing up to do a task. Members' relationship with God and each other faded in importance," Baumann wrote.

Secondly, in the effort to get parishioners to sign up for the work of the parish, a "full menu" of existing slots was presented "with the expectation that people would immediately sign up to help in some area." The problem, as Baumann and other staff members gradually perceived and defined it, was that "there was little or no encouragement to offer a gift or share a dream for ministry. The unspoken message was that gifts of time and talent were expected to fit neatly into an existing parish task or ministry."

A third "unintended result," according to Baumann, was the "overwhelming amount of data generated by the "connecting process":

> Over one thousand forms were submitted, each with an average of five boxes checked, resulting in five thousand pieces of information to organize and distribute to the leaders of the various ministries. Even though parish members offered their time to accomplish this task—chaos reigned!

Efforts were made to develop a better use of the database, yet while this adjustment took place, ministry leaders were unable to add more potential volunteer names; moreover, parishioners who had committed to particular ministries were not contacted. A frustrating logjam was the consequence.

Fortunately, from Baumann's perspective, there were parish members who played the roles of "shepherds and wise men," jettisoning their plans and "making space" by reordering their lives to allow more time for family, a possibility that resulted from some people changing to jobs which paid less but which opened time for prayerful reflection and for choosing commitments with greater care—exemplifying the process of discernment.

The parish staff decided to put a hold on any new programs and activities. Rather than trying to fit new responsibilities into existing staff time, staffers waited until additional staff time was made available—in this case, by creating a new position into which John Baumann stepped, namely, directing stewardship formation. Baumann began to realize that as the parish moved into its basic facility in 1995, "two disparate communities" were emerging at St. John the Baptist. One was made up of original members who helped to develop the parish Stewardship Prayer and Ministry Statement. The other community included those who came just before and after the physical building was finished. Each group included the same number of families.

Baumann expressed the consequences of what he saw in the form of a lesson every stewardship parish should take to heart:

> The newer members had yet to grasp the concept of Stewardship on which the parish was founded. This "stewardship learning curve" takes about three to five years to fully grasp. Three distinct phases can be identified. First, members encounter the notion of stewardship as a new idea. Later, people make stewardship choices, have some experiences, and seek to grow and develop a stewardship response. Finally, members become fully engaged in discernment and stewardship, have made some discerned choices, and are growing into a lifestyle based on stewardship. This is not an end in the sense that growth and development stop, or members have achieved all there is to know about discernment and stewardship. It simply identifies a level of integration. This stewardship learning curve is a life-long experience based on our continued response to God's invitation to be in relationship with God.

For Baumann, this prayerful and reflective process of discernment is the saving alternative to the risks that often reside in earlier phases of a stewardship program: seemingly ceaseless rounds of planning, managing, and engineering. "The alternative paradigm of watching, making space, and gleaning news of the Incarnation, places an emphasis on relationship" [rather than planning, etc]. This paradigm can be developed to guide the parish ministry team in offering guidance to parish members "about how they might offer their gifts of time and talent."

In Retrospect

Father Walmesley is keenly aware of the advantage he and his parishioners had of starting anew, including that of having no church building. The consequence, he reflects, was an intentionality shared by members. Nothing outward attracted them—certainly not the metal chairs the school provided and the schoolbooks along the wall. "The only people who came were those who really wanted to. And we could build on that. Our stewardship became an intentional way of life; it had more resonance than it might in a more established church."

Father Walmesley acknowledges that it will be a challenge to keep stewardship as "the driving force." One way is to continue reinforcing stewardship in the parish liturgies:

> Each Sunday we try to do some ritual with the offering baskets. During the stewardship campaign in the fall, we do it with music as well. Once again, I make a point of bringing the baskets into the offertory prayer, "Blessed are You, Lord God of all creation," the idea being, we thank You for these generous gifts today, for the work and ministry of your church. Something as simple as that. People began to notice: Rather than being pushed to one side, put away as though it were dirty and let's get back to the Mass, the money offerings represent what you and I give back to God. So we do that pretty well.

High and consistent intentionality is a key to understanding the success enjoyed by St. John the Baptist Parish. The spelling out of what stewardship means in the 1992 Stewardship Program brochure, with concrete illustrations of expected giving levels and hours of volunteering, dispels any "fuzziness" about what joining this parish entails. Stewardship is given concrete, explicit meaning. It is far from an abstract, high-sounding theological utterance. It asks for a definite commitment, which a majority of parishioners are willing to give.

Not least remarkable is the continuing high level of giving. In 1996 Father Walmesley remarked to me that as numerical growth continues, percentage of those giving declines. This seems not to have been the case at St. John the Baptist. Giving percentages remain high, as is made clear in the complimentary letter from the director of the archdiocesan Revolving Fund.

Parish success is in no small degree attributable, I think, to persistent and creative efforts to impart a sense of ownership. Seeking consensus in the many ways indicated above ensured strong support for the capital campaign that ensued. No small cadre of top parish leaders, no semi-closed parish council engineered these decisions. They truly emanated "from the ground up." Open disclosure was central to the entire consensus-seeking enterprise. Parish liturgies, in turn, reflected this sense of a community "on the march," growing in faith as it expanded in size.

New member gatherings became a most effective avenue of recruiting parish volunteers, again conferring an expectation that if you belong to this parish, you will be asked to consider serving. And few parishes are clearer in outlining what their organizations and ministries are about than St. John the Baptist. Today the parish boasts of seventy-five ministries.

Finally, the ideal of stewardship is reiterated throughout all these processes and strategies. It is no vague concept in this parish. Yet this very ideal also led thoughtful parish leaders like John Baumann on the path of discernment, recognizing how easily parish members get caught up in the frenetic, seemingly ceaseless lifestyles that can work their way into ministry volunteering. Perhaps at an advanced stage of stewardship, this kind of risk must be addressed. John Baumann's carefully crafted paradigm of "watching, making space" and becoming "shepherds and wise men" is almost a prophetic warning to soften the pace and listen. One is led back to the bishops' quotation from spiritual writer Frederick Buechner, speaking of one's calling:

> . . . maybe that is the place to start: the business of listening and hearing. [One's] life is full of all sorts of voices calling him [her] in all sorts of directions. Some of them are voices from inside and some of them are voices from outside. The more alive and alert we are, the more clamorous our lives are. Which do we listen to? What kind of voice do we listen for?"[2]

---

[2] Ibid., 18.

Chapter 7

A Traditional Church
with a Modern Message

THE BASILICA OF SAINT MARY
MINNEAPOLIS, MINNESOTA

"If you're writing about stewardship," a friend advised, "don't pass up the Basilica in Minneapolis." I was not about to. Fresh in mind was a presentation by four members of the Basilica staff at the 1997 International Catholic Stewardship Conference. Two years later I listened to them again at a regional stewardship conference in Spokane. By the fall of 1999 the Basilica had taken two first-place awards from the International Catholic Stewardship Council, one for "Total Capital Campaign Effort," another for "Video for a Parish Stewardship Appeal." A visit to Minneapolis in late August 1999 validated what I had heard. This is indeed an outstanding parish.

The very word "basilica" suggests a large church. Technically, a basilica is a rectangular building with a semi-circular apse on one end. But it is also a special Vatican designation that permits a seal, a coat of arms, and certain ceremonial privileges. Begun in 1907 and completed in 1914, the church was named America's first basilica by Pope Pius XI in 1926. In 1967 the Basilica was designated co-Cathedral of the Archdiocese of St. Paul and Minneapolis, sharing the honor with the Cathedral of St. Paul, which was designed by the same French architect, Emmanuel Masqueray (1861–1917). It was added to the National Register of Historic Places in 1975.

The Basilica is far more than an impressive architectural treasure that attracts visitors year round. A vital, active presence in the city, its membership has grown phenomenally from approximately fifteen hundred households in 1990 to over forty-eight hundred in 2000. Even more remarkable is a demographic profile showing 70 percent of the Basilica's registered members are under the age of 45, and 77 percent have a college or postgraduate degree. Nearly 75 percent work in managerial or technical fields. A visitor can't miss the enthusiasm of priests, staff, committee chairs and members, the proliferation of ministries, the excellence of liturgical worship and music, and the church's strong affirmation by the greater Minneapolis community as evidenced by support given to a recent capital campaign. The Basilica is indeed no ordinary parish.

Stewardship:
The Basic Commitment

Stewardship has become a central motivating force in the Basilica's growth both financially and in the number of volunteers during the 1990s. The pastor, ministry directors, and committees share a commitment to its ideals, but four key people appear to play major roles in the articulation and implementation of stewardship: Father Michael J. O'Connell, rector of the Basilica since 1991; Tom Green, director of Finance and Administration; Chris Okey, chair of the Stewardship Committee; Chris Deets, chair of the Creative Stewardship Committee. Each has his own angle of vision and personal emphasis.

Father Michael J. O'Connell

Ordained in 1967, Father O'Connell can look back on pastoral experience covering a lot of territory. He became acquainted in the early 1980s with Francis ("Dutch") and Barbara Scholtz, who subsequently became perhaps the best-known sacrificial giving and stewardship advocates in the country. After the Scholtzes moved to Florida in 1988, he would meet them again as he attended International Catholic Stewardship Conferences. Sacrificial giving and stewardship were familiar ideals when he became the Basilica's rector in 1991. He and Tom Green, who was hired as director of Finance and Administration in 1989, began to seek strategies for increasing giving. By the mid-1990s, Father O'Connell explained:

I began attending the national conference because I wanted to renew my own sense of the spiritual realm of stewardship. It was very helpful to go back and reconnect. Now, along with my primary responsibility to preach the Word, celebrate the Eucharist, and articulate the parish vision and mission, I know I'm [also] to articulate the theology and spirituality of stewardship. I do it all the time, trying to find creative ways of teaching and preaching. I carry the theme into committee meetings as well. I see stewardship [as] giving gratefully and generously of the gifts God has given us, including time, talent, and treasure, as a way of life, in fact, a way of liberating the soul from the lethal culture of consumerism. Regarding stewardship of money, I don't hesitate to talk about it. My father was a salesman. He had me out selling pots and pans when I was fifteen, door to door. It was really tough. What I learned was, if you believe in your product and you believe it can give purpose and pleasure to other people, then why would you even hesitate to ask them to buy it? And if they say no, it's not personal. I learned that from my dad too. Even deeper than that, if some of the rejections of what you're selling get personal, that's their problem, not yours! All this may sound crass as a metaphor, but I am selling the best thing that anybody could buy. I am also selling something this culture is desperately hungry for. And if the crassness is to imply that it costs something, well, I happen to believe that it *does* cost something, just like Dietrich Bonhoeffer's great book, *The Cost of Discipleship*. There ain't no free lunch. Anything that is worth anything *costs*. It costs time, energy, money. And nobody is selling anything more valuable than the gospel of Jesus Christ. So it really doesn't occur to me to apologize or feel the least bit guilty or shameful or hesitant to say to somebody, "Hey, you want to invest in something that is absolutely wonderful, that will help you and others?" Why not? Compared to the other things we invest in, why not this? If I do so, I am giving you the key to liberation from the tyranny of possessions, from the tyranny of the *illusion* of security. I invite you to consider that these things are all gifts meant for the common good along with my individual good. The sociologist Robert N. Bellah pointed out in a recent timely article in America ["Religion and the Shape of National Culture," July 1999] that Catholicism, in its doctrine of sin and redemption, takes a much more positive view of society and its capability of redemption and renewal. The common good is positive—we go to *communion*, you see. The fundamental theological premise is that we are saved in the Body of Christ. As Bellah says, though, "If there is anything this country can learn now and needs to learn, [it] is how the Catholic

Church holds out the hope that cultivating the corporate and common good can make a difference—the contribution of individual gifts of time and talent and money for the common good."

You seem to carry this notion of the common good into your work with parish committees by really listening to them.

Well, take the Parish Council. It advises me primarily as mission- and vision- and values-keeper. We are a very mission- and values-driven parish. Our vision is taken from Jeremiah 29, "Work for the good of the city to which I have exiled you; pray to Yahweh on its behalf, since on its welfare yours depends"[JB]. That reaches over everything. All three committees, Finance and Stewardship added in, together with the Executive Committee of our capital campaign, make up a force field guided by annual overall goals reflecting our mission and vision, strategic priorities. These goals are for the overall good of the parish and are delivered by me and the key managers. And the Parish Council's job, with me, is to form a litmus test, a template, applied on a regular basis: Is the operation of this parish faithful to its mission, vision, values, and strategic plan? Of course, you have to remember that each parish's concept of the working of those three committees is *sui generis*, reflecting the particular character of that community.

Do you consider stewardship to involve a countercultural stance?

Well, I think we have to remember that seldom in the history of the Church has there been so much defining and redefining of the Church in such a short period of time. I think the Church has succeeded where it has been a countercultural force. That's what the gospel is. On the other hand, "I did not come to condemn this world but to fulfill the will of my Father." So in terms of the ministry, message, and method of Jesus, you have to be perfectly clear on what it is about this culture that is basically going to take your life from you—holding up a mirror, but not in such a way as to condemn you or put you in a position so off-putting that all you want to do is fight with me. If I'm sitting in a tavern with you talking to you about this culture so that it really makes you look into the mirror, look at what's entered in your check register, but I'm still having a drink *with* you—you see, that's what the Church is talking about in terms of running counter to the culture. It's what the Church has to do—to be with people as they hear a message that's painful but also liberating. Too often, though, we're just throwing marshmallows.

Tom Green

Tom's background was made to order for the position of director of Finance and Administration at the Basilica. While working his way up the corporate ladder at J.C. Penney Co., he managed a succession of stores in the Twin Cities area, the last one in downtown Minneapolis. A corporate decision to close the store in 1986 forced Tom into a brief period of unemployment involving soul-searching and a reevaluation of priorities. Following his employment with J.C. Penney, Tom held several jobs, including teaching retail management at the University of Minnesota. He was hired at the Basilica in 1989.

Attending annual meetings of the International Catholic Stewardship Council turned Tom into an enthusiastic convert. Stewardship wasn't easy to start up in the early 1990s, he acknowledges. The original committee began with three or four members. By 1999 it had fifteen, increasing to eighteen by mid-2000. "Everyone's aboard now," he remarks. As we shall see in a subsequent interview, recruiting of time and talent is very well organized at the Basilica. "We're constantly inviting people to consider volunteering for ministry. When I first came in 1989, we had fewer than four hundred volunteers. Now we have over thirty-three hundred."

As his title suggests, Tom is highly focused on the financial well-being at Saint Mary's. One innovation that truly stands out has attracted interest wherever the "Basilica team" is invited to speak:

> We've taken a marketing approach through our brochures and our pledge form. We are also strong advocates of electronic giving. We have six hundred parishioners using this method [as of 1999]. We've found that the average electronic gift is ten to thirteen dollars per week higher than the normal stewardship pledges. We believe strongly that this is the wave of the future.

By 2001, 37 percent of total dollars pledged annually were contributed electronically from parishioners' bank accounts. Tom Green highlights the advantage to the parish of steady, predictable income each month, noting further that the 32 percent increase of automatic-pledgers in 1998 over the previous year did not come mainly from regular pledgers to the parish. It was spread across the membership and included people who had never pledged or even contributed before. Electronic pledgers, while making up only 12 percent of the parish's forty-eight hundred households, accounted for over 20 percent of the parish's weekly income. As Tom points out to parishioners, "It's easy, it's convenient, and it's very important."

Tom takes a fatherly pride in the talented young parishioners who contribute their skills to the parish. A striking example is how the parish quarterly, *Basilica* magazine, evolved:

> About five years ago we decided to do something about our drab-looking church bulletin. No pizazz to it. We put out an appeal for creative people to come forward to help improve the bulletin. About twenty-two people responded to that call, giving up two hours every Friday night, February through May. Now the bulletin looks great and is mailed out rather than just being distributed in church. These volunteers included graphic designers, photographers, writers, and production people. One of these young people suggested maybe we weren't thinking big enough, being visionary in our communication with parishioners and to the greater community around us. He proposed a quarterly magazine much like alumni organizations send out. Eventually the entire committee said, "Yes, we can do this—a magazine educating everyone about programs offered within the Basilica." We went to a printer, a friend of Father Michael's, not even a parishioner. Would he be willing to do the work on a pro bono basis? He said, "I totally respect what's going on in the Basilica, its programs for the greater community. We'll help you do it." So for the last five years we've put out a thoroughly professional magazine—stories, programs, new staff members' profiles, what we're doing for the greater community. It's been a tremendous part of our overall success. Many who started the magazine have remained with it.

Tom takes a personal interest in employment ministry. A profile of him in *Basilica* included these words:

> "Six months out of work gave me great insights into wanting to make a difference for the unemployed." Thanks in part to this first-hand experience, he now focuses on leveraging his contacts in the business community to help find new jobs for unemployed and underemployed parishioners.[1]

---

[1] "Tom Terrific: Administrator Tom Green's Commitment Goes Beyond Superlatives," *Basilica* (Summer 1996) 19.

Tom later reminded me that the employment program is for *anyone* who asks for help, not only for those attending the Basilica:

> This is part of the way a church should reach out to its community and not just for registered parishioners. People of all kinds come here for this assistance. We're here to serve their needs as well as we can, whether they're Jewish, Protestant, Lutheran, or Catholic. That's really the spirit we have here.

More broadly, Father O'Connell believes that a key to effective stewardship, and a reason why the staff set out to improve the parish bulletin and create the magazine, is constantly and creatively to remind "customers" *how well* their contributions of time and talent are actually doing. Precisely because they contribute, the Basilica is changing and saving lives. This is the good news resulting from proclaiming the Good News.

Tom is also proud of the parish endowment begun in 1998, which reached $250,000 by the fall of 1999. Neither principal nor interest was to be touched "until it hits a million dollars. We want it dedicated to the upkeep of our marvelous facility. We've just started, but the potential is enormous. We're only at the tip of the iceberg now."

Tom's innate optimism convinces him that things are only going to get better at the Basilica, that stewardship ideals carry unlimited potential:

> Bottom line is that we're constantly pushing the envelope to find innovative ways of serving the people both in our parish community and in the greater community. It's this that really makes us tick—this plus our tremendous outreach, our welcoming attitude, and our encouragement of people to get involved in ministry with us. It's this very involvement that is bringing more and more volunteers into action in serving all God's children.

Chris Okey

The Stewardship Committee functions as one of several subcommittees of the Finance Committee; another is the Budget Subcommittee, of which Chris is also a member, while chairing the Stewardship Committee. The role of the latter is to help facilitate the growth of stewardship in the parish. According to Chris:

The committee is trying to change the culture. We're the envisioning committee, figuring out what it means to be a steward who gives of time and talent. I've tried to bring into the parish my own program-manager model at Honeywell, which involves some aggressive planning. Then I have to remind myself that this is God's work and requires a different mindset. Oh sure, if this were a business, I'd have open communication among all the committees we've been talking about—the whole process better defined, with each committee, or at least the chairs, reading the materials of the other committees, and then a forum for communication among the chairs. Now, a lot of that occurs informally within the hallways here or at conversations after Mass. We're moving toward better-defined forms of communication. At work I'm used to standing up and saying, "We need this now," and usually getting a positive response. It's slower in a parish, very definitely. However, the key is to focus on the progress made and stay with it year after year.

A prime objective, Chris reflects, is to bring the message of stewardship closer to the parish:

That's where our Creative Stewardship Subcommittee comes in. Its members are really skilled in bringing home a message—talented marketers, writers, graphic artists, and so on. Last year we came up with the idea of "initiatives." In these, a committee member has to take the leadership and look at a specific issue. Appreciated securities are an example. How do we bring this form of gift-giving to more parishioners? Now, we have this motivated member experienced in the securities industry who wants to pursue this idea, which is a very appropriate initiative for a stewardship committee. I know you've been told about electronic giving, which is an early, very successful initiative. The key to our success is that Father Michael does attend our meetings, but he's just like a member. He receives deference, of course, but his motions can get tabled and he can be outvoted and overridden! Finally, to keep us all rooted, we are planning a retreat, where we will focus on stewardship in our own lives.

The influence of Chris Okey and the other young professionals on the Stewardship Committee is apparent in the organized, task-based approach they take. In a handout dated August 1, 1999, the division of labor between the full Stewardship Committee and the Creative Stewardship Committee was succinctly set down: The former's charge was "direction" and "market segments"; for the latter, "content" and "message."

Tables 1 and 2 (see pages 122 and 123) are taken from the 1999–2000 Stewardship Campaign document and show how committee tasks were framed in terms of "Goals" and "Tools." This living document will be updated as the campaign progresses. Consider a key statement under "Goals": "Our task is to translate our primary Stewardship goal into smaller, more specific, and measurable goals and to define strategies to achieve these goals." Such an approach has the merit of being concrete and definite and, while leaving room for discussion at any point, leaves no member in doubt as to what is being proposed. Once agreed upon, every strategy stands with its means of implementation, whether it is letters sent out, phone calls, suggested themes for homilies, etc. Nothing is hazy or "fuzzy." Increasing the proportion of pledgers is obviously a central goal, since deciding to pledge, a highly intentional act, usually has the effect on the parishioner of raising the amount given at a previous level.

Chris Deets

A writer of advertising copy by profession, Chris is typical of the talented young professionals drawn to the work of the Basilica. He recalled a moment when his faith and the ideals of stewardship took on new life. In the course of writing an article for the *Basilica* magazine on stewardship, he interviewed "a gentleman who talked about his faith not as a noun but as a verb, as something he invokes in his daily life." Chris was struck as the man related that if he gives more than he can afford to the church that week, he doesn't know how he will make it through that week. Yet his faith tells him he will, and he always comes through. He was so convinced of what he was saying, Chris went on, it was almost like a conversion:

> . . . someone has an effect on you and they change you. That's what really happened to me. Since then I've reflected on faith not as a noun but as a verb and on priorities. I saw that stewardship is exercising choice and making a priority. That itself requires faith, faith in action. So, "Are you faithful?" means "Is your faith active?" Even more deeply is the idea that we're not in control of our lives, not the creator; we have zero control over our lives—a belief that itself requires faith. Translating this into stewardship, if you're

TABLE 1

Goals

Our primary Steward goal for the 1999–2000 campaign is:

Increase in total dollars pledged from the 1998–99 Campaign by 15%.

There are three ways in which we can achieve this goal:
1. Increase in total number of current parishioners pledging,
2. Increase the amount pledged by members,
3. Add parishioners to the parish who pledge.

Our task is to translate our primary Stewardship goal into smaller, more specific, and measurable goals and to define strategies to achieve these goals.

Increase the number of appreciated securities pledges from X% to Y%

Goal	Strategy
Increase the number of pledgers from X% to Y%	To be decided by September Stewardship Meeting
Increase the number of new members pledging from X% to Y%	To be decided by September Stewardship Meeting
Increase the number of appreciated securities pledges from X% to Y%	To be decided by September Stewardship Meeting
Convert two-years and older, consistent, weekly, or monthly givers into pledgers	Send a set of specific letters to these givers with the following suggested messages: • Come home, back into the fold • Thank you for your loyal giving
Move under two-years old, consistent, and sporadic givers into pledgers	Send a set of specific letters to these givers with the following suggested messages: • Thanks for joining • Become a full member and pledge
Convert nongivers who are actively involved in volunteer activities into pledgers	Send a set of specific letters to these givers with the following suggested messages: • Thanks for your commitment • Wouldn't you please consider extending your commitment to a financial gift

TABLE 2

Tools

The following are the typical tools that we use to reach our parishioners. It is these tools that form the basis of our strategies to reach our goals. Some of the tools are only broad reaching, while some can be targeted toward a specific audience.

No.	Tool	Required Consultation outside of the Stewardship Committees
1	Letters	—
2	Home Visits	—
3	Pledge card message	—
4	In church material (i.e., pew, back of church, ushers, banners, etc.)	Liturgical Director
5	Stewardship Outreach (telethon)	—
6	Lay witness speakers	Liturgical Director
7	Homilies	Liturgical Director
8	Brief pulpit "asks" (e.g., at the end of a homily, or at announcement)	Liturgical Director
9	Bulletin	—
10	*Basilica* magazine	Magazine Committee
11	Stewardship brochure	—
12	Theme	—
13	Video	—
14	Web site	—

asked to volunteer for something, to give of your talents, you *do that*. And you make a leap of faith that you *do* have the time or that you *are* a good writer, or if you give *first*, you will be given enough to get you through until the next time you give. You will be taken care of.

Reflecting on communicating with his contemporaries, Chris notes that it is indeed important to quote scriptural passages and use the vocabulary of stewardship. But just staying with a traditional vocabulary

really doesn't resonate as much as saying things like, "What are your priorities? Does your money go to your car? Time go to your friends? Talent go only into your work?" This is a contemporary context. That's the challenge, sort of a tightrope you have to walk— and the Basilica walks it everyday. Take our magazine. It looks so contemporary, yet the message communicated has been around for two thousand years. The magazine uses twentieth-century technology to deliver a message that transcends the ages. What a fabulous combination!

The *Basilica* quarterly, Chris says, prompts the staff to come up with an advertising campaign for stewardship that is "light, with humor, but also with reverence and acknowledging the sacred. Some people don't think these can be combined, but they can." In his view, stewardship should not be viewed as something one *has* to do or is pushed to do.

Tom Green talks about this a lot. Take the idea of stewardship as priorities and apply it to your own life. If you're thinking about giving, you have to take away something from your life. Well, you *choose* what you want to take away. If you want to give up a latte every day or a movie a week, okay, apply it and do it.

Chris agrees with those who believe that Catholic priests talk too seldom about money. Everyone else out there in the culture, he reflected, is ready to "tell you how your pie should be sliced up."

That's the unfortunate thing about the Catholic Church: Not enough people tell us how big a slice should go to our Faith. The United Way has no trouble coming into my place of work and telling me how much I should donate. But priests seem to have a tremendous amount of trouble telling us how much should go to our Faith. I don't mean "give 100 percent." They really don't have to say how much; rather, at what point do you give *first?* And you should give *first* to your church or to your Faith. I'm convinced, if they preached that message—your time, talent, treasure should go to your church first—they would help people do what most of us don't, that is, think or reflect about spending. No one ever stops you and says, "Think about how you spend your money."

At the Basilica there is no hesitancy about using Scripture and faith to alert parishioners to their obligation to give to their church and to reflect on how they spend their money. Hopefully, in so doing, in a prayerful manner, their generosity will increase toward the Basilica, whose arms stretch out to help all in need.

Stewardship of Treasure

In the early 1990s, increasing regular giving to the Basilica of Saint Mary was a true challenge for pastor and staff. While the parish was steadily growing in numbers and volunteers in the 1990s, giving lagged behind. Partly responsible, as we shall see, was a huge capital campaign to save the church and develop the undercroft of the church. Chris Deets commented incisively:

> As the parish grew by over 18 percent in 1996, stewardship pledges dropped by 12 percent. On top of that, 21 percent of the parish gave less than 98 cents a week, and 40 percent gave no financial support. The result: when the books were closed June 30, 1996, the Basilica had a deficit of over $20,000.[2]

Accompanying charts dramatized the situation:

> If each parish household increased its giving by the cost of one six-pack of soda, income at the Basilica would increase in 1997 by $613,756.
>
> —$7.00 or the cost of a feature movie (increase of $1,346,800)
>
> —$2.96 for a video rental (increase of $596,504)
>
> —$1.80 for a large cappuccino (increase of $346,320)

[2] Chris Deets, "Financial Stewardship: Greater Commitment Needed to Ease Budget Concerns," *Basilica* (Autumn 1996) 7.

Average weekly giving per household was listed on another chart:

—a local Lutheran parish ($28.50)

—a Presbyterian church ($16.23)

—a Methodist congregation ($14.84)

—even another Catholic parish ($9.80)

At the bottom was Basilica of Saint Mary at $6.77.

Perhaps most telling, another chart listed the percentages of the parish community by age in one column with its average weekly offering in an adjoining column. Top giving went to those 60 to 69 years old ($18.23), who constituted a mere 4.93 percent of the parish. A painful contrast was evident in the younger groups: 40–49 ($6.15); 30–39 ($3.31); and 20–29 ($.98), who together made up two-thirds of parish membership. In this context Father O'Connell's words hit home sharply:

> The heart of stewardship is commitment. It's taking ownership in this community. When you give to the Basilica, you are saying, "I value this place and all it adds to my life, and I'm committed to supporting it.

Tom Green weighed in as well:

> Our greatest challenge here is educating people about the need for a commitment to stewardship. I'm asking that people look at their budget, and then look at the Basilica's budget. Some people may not have another penny to give. But others will see that they can increase their giving substantially. . . . We are under-budgeting to match our income. As a result, we're not offering the kind of services we should be offering to our community.

This stark exhortation evidently hit home. The next fiscal year saw giving go up by 16 percent. While this was welcome news, the 1997 stewardship report homed in on the number of people *pledging*. Entitled "Commitment—The Gift Only You Can Give," the report noted that although the parish had nearly doubled in size since 1995, just 34 percent of parishioners made a pledge at the start of 1997. Following appropriate scriptural quotations, the report framed a basic pledging message to everyone:

> Pledging your stewardship is commitment in its highest form. It's your personal partnership with God; giving your word to support His word. It's saying yes to your faith. A *yes* only you can say. When you say *yes* to stewardship, you say *yes* to the fundamental belief that as you support God, He will support you. Ask yourself, "Is this something I believe?" Your answer reflects the depth of your faith.

Again, an accompanying chart noted that a Presbyterian, a Methodist, and a Lutheran church in the Twin Cities had, respectively, 54 percent, 50 percent, and 37 percent of parishioners pledging as of May 1997.

The strong message approach seemed to pay off. Financial gifts in the fiscal year 1997–1998 rose nearly 20 percent. The percentage of households pledging rose to 36 percent, including 8 percent who pledged electronically. While another 22 percent of parish households contributed without pledging, their average weekly gift amounted to only $3.34 as compared with approximately $17 per week by those pledging. Yet this still left 42 percent of households not contributing anything.

A weighty decision was made for the fiscal year 1998–1999: The Basilica would combine its capital and annual stewardship campaigns. For the first time volunteers would call on individual households to explain the church's campaign goals. The proposed budget of $1.9 million called for another 18 percent increase in regular or stewardship giving. At this point we turn to the capital campaign for restoration and developing of the Basilica's undercroft.

The Capital Campaign

Since the Basilica has received a national award for its capital campaign, a word about its scope seems called for. The Basilica had fallen into such disrepair by the 1980s that thought was given to closing it. In 1989 about $250,000 went into emergency repairs. In 1990 a campaign began to continue restoration, which also included development of the church's undercroft for badly needed additional space. However, in the words of Teresa (Terri) Ashmore, hired as director of Development in 1993, "It kind of stalled out as the Basilica underwent a change of pastors." Terri's job was to restart the campaign. Her previous work was in the Minnesota political sector—helping to find candidates, raise money, and get them elected. An early high-priority task was to get the pastor involved:

Now Father O'Connell grew up in St. Paul, and in this community the river is the dividing line. So he didn't know a lot of the downtown Minneapolis CEOs—people from the western suburbs who are Catholic as well. We also knew that money couldn't come from the parish alone. So we did an aggressive outreach, getting Father to have lunch or coffee with Catholic community leaders to talk about this vision and the Basilica's mission. Following this, Chris Rahill of the Creative Stewardship Committee came up with the idea of a Basilica Alumni Society. Keep in mind that the Basilica was growing fast each year and that very many new members were young (under forty) and were college graduates. Giving to their alumni associations was probably their first experience of connecting to and giving to an institution they appreciated. We wanted to capture that—the feeling of alumni taking care of an institution. So we talked about "The Classes of 1994, 1995, 1996," etc. We did things typical of an alumni association: wearables, watches, t-shirts, some little premiums that were not too expensive—all to give them some sense of identification with the church. Add to this inviting people into church for wine and cheese receptions, very inexpensive. Father Michael talked to them about what we were doing and why their help was so valuable. We followed up by mail and phone solicitations.

A broad appeal was made based on the importance of the role of the Basilica in the community—its outreach to the poor as well as strong liturgy and educational ministries:

For parishioners, we talked about what we as a church could do in the community. On the outside, we told them why they should help save the Basilica, because without it the community would not be as nice a place. Then we had events. Some were for "high-end audiences," people who could spend $500 or $1,000 to hear *The Messiah*. Other events were for families with children, for example, tickets for the St. Paul Saints baseball games.

The biggest event, and one for which the Basilica is noted far beyond Minneapolis, was the annual "Block Party," begun in 1995. This two-day event, featuring live rock bands, involved fifteen hundred, mostly young, volunteers. It has become a major fund-raising vehicle, growing each year and contributing hundreds of thousands of dollars toward the capital campaign fund.

Terri Ashmore accepted Tom Green's invitation to attend the annual International Catholic Stewardship Conference:

> . . . where I started to learn about the theology of stewardship. In fund-raising, we refer to "case"—what's your "case" for soliciting donations? Here I find stewardship's "case" very challenging, the best in the world. I started without a clue. But as you learn about stewardship, it's a way of challenging yourself spiritually.

A big decision, of course, was to run the 1998–1999 stewardship and capital campaigns together.

> Very challenging. Very scary. We needed $6,300,000 for the undercroft church basement development, $2.2 million coming from the parish. Two hundred volunteers called on nine hundred people personally in the parish. And we succeeded. From last November till today [September 1999] we did raise $5,000,000 both from within the parish and outside. In addition, $1,600,000 was raised for the parish itself, the regular stewardship appeal. Remember that it took us seven years to raise $7,000,000 in the first phase! Now it's a different feeling. People really care about this place and want it to continue what it has been doing. We had tours of the facility we wanted to develop. One of our rallying cries was "Put bathrooms in the church!" Really, we don't have bathrooms anywhere in the church, nor kitchen facilities. And so many groups can't find meeting space.

Did pairing the two solicitations work? While underlining the obvious success of the capital campaign, Terri Ashmore pointed out that stewardship giving did go up by 7 percent, but this fell short of the 15 percent increase anticipated to accommodate rapid growth of the parish. "So the depressing effect was in the size of the increase [to fund the parish budget]."

An Update

Tom Green termed the 2000 stewardship campaign "a tremendous success." Aided by the Creative Stewardship Committee's eye-catching stewardship brochure, pledge form, and envelope, the parish experienced a 23 percent increase (320 additional pledgers) over 1999. A record

41 percent of households were now pledging. Total dollars pledged came to $1,765,000, a 23 percent increase over 1999. Electronic pledgers rose from 430 in 1999 to 533 in 2000, a 24 percent increase. Moreover, Tom said, "Our first-year parishioners (we fondly refer to them as our 'Class of 1999') are committing to stewardship quicker and giving at a higher percentage than the rest of our parish."

As mentioned above, the parish has for several years featured New Member Dinners, at which recently registered parishioners learn about opportunities for giving and for volunteering. Expanding on this, Tom said:

> Now we've started to do a quarterly Sunday brunch for new members. They are very well attended. This immediate form of welcoming and hospitality is key to our overall success. We've had about two hundred new households join our parish in the last ten months.

Dedication of the new undercroft took place on June 3 and 4, 2000. "The total cost of our undercroft development will be $6.3 million dollars. We expect to be totally pledged out within ninety days" [by August 2000]. Father O'Connell's message, "The Miracle of Your Stewardship," attached to the stewardship pledge form, admirably links the call for financial commitment with the Basilica's mission:

> Stewardship isn't just about writing a check. It's about making a commitment. It's about sharing gifts God has given us and receiving all the love and help and spiritual strength of a vibrant faith community. Imagine what the Basilica would be without stewardship. Think how our faith community would change if we no longer reached out to the poor, the lonely, and the spiritually hungry. What if we suddenly stopped teaching children about the love of God? Picture a liturgy without music . . . a Mass without hospitality . . . grief without support. All that and so much more is made possible only by stewardship. Our gifts from God have made our lives better than they could otherwise have been. Please consider how important your stewardship is to the mission of the Basilica. It is truly one of our everyday miracles. A pledge of any amount is always meaningful to the Basilica. Typically, our parishioners make weekly pledges between 2 percent to 10 percent of their weekly income. Use the chart below to determine a pledge that is suitable to your household. Then apply that amount as you fill out the adjacent pledge form. *Please be as generous as possible!*

Stewardship of Time and Talent

The Basilica's extraordinary number of volunteers and long list of ministries reflect a tradition of activism. Msgr. Terrance Berntson returned from the Second Vatican Council with enthusiasm for more lay involvement, including women assuming leadership roles in the parish. As pastor, he encouraged formation of the Care Guild, which began with forty women in 1974. Within three months membership had reached 128, with five standing committees supporting both existing and new ministries: Membership and Parish Newcomers; Spiritual and Cultural Enrichment; Social Action; Hospital, Nursing Homes and Home-bound; Fund-Raising and Parish Needs. Along with a Food Shelf in the rectory basement, Guild activities by the mid-1970s had expanded in all directions:

> The sewing group made crafts to sell at Fun Fest and the Christmas Boutique; they collected Christmas gifts for parishioners in nursing homes; volunteers worked the Aquatennial crowds, selling popcorn, snow cones, and other goodies; they presented flowers to each mother attending Mass on Mother's Day; and they gave Thanksgiving baskets to the needy, filled partly by the proceeds of pumpkin sales in October. Newcomer receptions saw as many as fifty people attending. The Marriage Encounter program was introduced, and a young adults group was organized . . . spiritual and social opportunities . . . included activities such as Lenten programs, book discussions, retreats, musical concerts, and tours of the Minneapolis Institute of Art. . . .[3]

The Guild no longer exists, but its legacy is amply evident in the seventy-one ministries now supported by the Basilica and its two thousand-plus volunteers. While space precludes a description of each, Sue Hayes, director of Volunteer Ministry, gave us an overview. An entry point for many parish volunteers, she pointed out, is the annual summer Block Party: "Our younger members often come to us through the party." First-time attendees often migrate to other ministries and eventually to parish committees. Not all become registered parish members right away, but often service in a ministry leads to eventual registration and full membership in the parish. Sue described the steps her office goes through:

[3] Deanna Campbell, "A Lasting Legacy: Many Basilica Ministries Have Roots in the Care Guild," *Basilica* (Spring 1997) 17.

I feel overwhelmed at times by the unsolicited daily phone calls from people who want to help and become involved. My office makes available a time and talent folder, in which ministries are listed under several headings. A response card is included. Once filled out, it comes to me. I then fill out a form for heads of ministries, who will be doing follow-up phone calls. I enter the interests people expressed into our database. They then receive a letter acknowledging that I have received their card, their interests have been noted, and that a person will be contacting them within two weeks.

Do you have enough ministry slots for all the people interested?

True, some areas don't have an immediate need for people. In those cases people are notified that they may go on a waiting list. But many check more than one slot, and I can go to that. Let me say, though, that recruiting is not our biggest challenge. Placement and training are. For example, our director of Pastoral Ministry has gradually developed a befriending ministry and a ministry to the elderly. We have identified a number of parishioners over eighty. For the last year, she has been recruiting and training volunteers and now is ready for them to begin. In a parish this size, clergy alone cannot meet pastoral care needs.

Have you thought of term limits for members of ministries and committees?

We have, but it hasn't been enforced in any way. I worked with department heads last year to develop job descriptions for each position. Term limits are supposed to be written in to these. Some heads, so far, choose to fill that in; others don't. I do want staff to think about this issue, though, because we do need to encourage more people to enter ministries.

You hear people speak of "the 80-20 principle." Has this parish transcended that?

Well, I know the list I'm now working on for the annual report has 2,156 names on it. That would include volunteers for the Block Party; right now there are fourteen to fifteen hundred alone! The rest are involved in other ministries. And many are involved in more than one. Also, I don't know how many on the list are actually registered parishioners. Then we have low-intensity events like the parish picnic, which may involve fifty to sixty people. But once it's over, that's it. Another entry point besides the Block Party is our information desk at the rear of the church after every liturgy. A hospitality desk is there, too, where people can meet one another and get cards for ministry sign-ups. At each liturgy the presider will announce that people may register afterwards. Another entry point for volunteers is decorating the church. Teams form for each liturgical season or specific holidays. We [can] easily sign up seventy people for events like these.

Sue Hayes believes firmly in the efficacy of personal invitations. Every new member who registers receives an invitation to the New Member Dinner, an occasion par excellence for "a personal touch." Along with making sure people have nametags at such events, Sue emphasizes:

> I really take notes as people introduce themselves, noting what they say as an aid to remembering who they are. I call every person who attends a New Member Dinner as a follow-up: "Do you have any questions?" Every month I get two or three calls, "Thanks for calling. I'd be interested in doing such and such." Realizing that not every new member could attend a Tuesday evening dinner, the parish introduced in June 1999 the new-member brunch following the 9:30 Sunday Mass.

Is there a focus on developing the ministry leadership talent of the parish young people?

> Temple Israel, with whom we have a good relationship, had a leadership development program for their young people. We tried that here in six sessions. We asked ministry heads to invite young people they knew had leadership potential. We invited seventy, and fifty came. Father O'Connell spoke. Topics were Vatican II; papal encyclicals that call for the laity to become more involved; prayer; and then a focus on leadership itself. We're now working on a series for next fall. Same theme: their role as Christian leaders. We have a good relationship with St. John's University at Collegeville, Minnesota, and various faculty members [come] on Wednesday evenings to lecture. Many of the young people who attended the four evenings two years ago are now in leadership positions in parish organizations and ministries, so we know it works. It's time to do it again.

It was clear that Sue Hayes enjoyed her job. She saw broad possibilities for expanding ministries and volunteers to staff them. Her concluding reflections could serve as a model for directors of ministry everywhere:

> My job entails taking wonderful, enthusiastic, generous people and finding a way for them to be involved which isn't just "filling slots." Rather, giv[ing] them a meaningful way to use their gifts and feel like they're making a contribution to the community, and having some fun, too, experiencing some gratification for what they're committing their time and talent to. There's a genuine need out there for people to do it. It's our job to find ways of allowing them to fill that need.

With just over seventy ministries and well over two thousand volunteers (and more signing up), clearly the Basilica has been very successful in a variety of ways. Personal attention to sign-up opportunities and follow-through with phone calls contribute to a sense of truly honoring the differing gifts within the parish.

Social Ministry

Janice Andersen, director of Social Ministry, sees her position as overseeing "faith in action," from providing direct services to advocating for social justice in trying to change institutions. Besides overseeing programs, Janice tries to integrate them into parish life, into the liturgy, "into all we do." She points immediately to the Basilica's St. Vincent de Paul ministry, with a yearly budget of nearly $225,000 and, in 1998, service to almost twelve thousand individuals. Its Shoe Ministry includes, along with vouchers for new shoes and gasoline, bus transportation, children's books, hats, gloves, and socks. Rectory Outreach embraces housing and employment assistance, referral and advocacy, food vouchers, and work-related clothing. Special Programs features back-to-school supplies, holiday baskets, and an Adopt-a-Family program at Christmas. A Disciple Ministry matches mentors with unemployed participants, helping the latter with time management, budgeting, workplace culture, and conflict management. A Jobs Task Force networks with community businesses to connect people with "appropriate, challenging jobs." An Education Task Force identifies community resources to ensure participants the skills, training, and education to help them prepare for a job.

Janice sees as one of her primary tasks getting volunteers to be reflective about what they are seeing and doing:

> Take our Shoe Ministry. Volunteers get face-to-face experience meeting people who live under the highways or in shelters. And it's non-threatening for them. It's a beginning. We're now striving for reflective time: "Okay, let's get deeper into this and understand what it's about. What questions did your experience raise?" Ideally, you'd like to have that reflective time right after the ministry experience. We've decided that a good idea is to bring volunteers together for a dinner and use that time to reflect on their experiences. The thing is, it's easy to get people to serve meals, give out shoe vouchers. The key is to get them to reflect and eventually get actively engaged in more long-term issues. Both men and women. I go to meetings of the local Association of Pastoral Ministers here in our area, almost all women. But we have a good mix of men and women in our outreach ministries. Social justice, after all, should involve everyone. I enjoy relating to downtown ministries involving other churches, such as the Metropolitan Interfaith Council on Affordable Housing (MICAH). There is a crisis here in affordable housing, as there is elsewhere. There are diversity issues as well. So building bridges is important in my job, leading to dialogue that will bring us to the point of conversion and openness.

When Janice became director in 1994, St. Vincent de Paul had what she terms an "ethos of faith that we do not actively raise money." The organization was in the red by $15,000. The parish responded positively but said, "Don't do that again. Be proactive with your fundraising." Now parishioner envelopes labeled "St. Vincent de Paul" bring in half its revenues. The remainder comes through a special collection and gifts, rent donations, children's book donations, and a gift from the parish.

While not a ministry of the Basilica itself, located across the street from the church is the Jeremiah Program, separate and outstanding in its own right. Inaugurated and supported by a partnership of downtown churches, schools, businesses, and local government, it provides housing and on-site child-care in a safe, structured environment for single mothers with children. But it does not stop there. The Jeremiah Program, with the help of volunteers, also provides job training and counseling to assist mothers in deciding which educational programs can best upgrade their skills. Within an easy bus commute or even walking distance to downtown Minneapolis are a host of educational institutions. The overall effect is to help residents actively participate in the workplace with living-wage jobs. It is precisely this kind of ministry that catches the attention of young men and women and motivates them to seek out other opportunities for service the Basilica may offer.

Educational Ministries

Children and youth formation is extensive, embracing a Sunday school that serves almost four hundred children with over thirty-five trained catechists aided by parent, adult, and youth volunteers. Occasional family Masses are planned by students and families, as are Advent and Lenten events. Marketplace: A Summer Family Faith Experience, features a living history of biblical times through drama, along with an actual marketplace.

Adult education is also extensive. The Basilica can call on faculty resources at St. John's University at Collegeville to support a "Theology Lecture Series." Featured in the fall of 1999 were such topics as "Beyond Words: The Bible and Its Role in Catholic Life," "The Eucharist and the Search for Community," and "The Human Person as Sacrament." Seven lectures on women's issues were also scheduled for 1999–2000, with such evocative titles as "Wintering: How Darkness Can Transform Our Lives," "Voices of Contemporary Women: Our Spiritual Legacy," and "Creating Your Spiritual Autobiography."

Catching my eye was a ministry called Catholics Coming Home, designed to help those ready to find their way back to Catholicism after years away. As one volunteer who had earlier gone through the program described it:

> It's like being part of an intentional community to work with the facilitators . . . and the other long-term volunteers. . . . People attend Catholics Coming Home because they are hurt or angry, or maybe they're just curious. It's a place for people to unburden themselves and hear sound theology, a place where people can come and learn and be healed. Going through the six-week program over and over is wonderful.[4]

[4] Francesca DiPiazza, "Joe Sulentich: Coming Home to Be Healed," *Basilica* (Winter 1998) 9.

In Retrospect

There is little doubt in my mind that the Basilica of Saint Mary is indeed, as so many I spoke with expressed it, "a really special place." Its dynamism is hard to attribute to any one feature. One, certainly, is accessibility. Situated in the middle of the metro area at the crossroads of two interstate highways, the Basilica's size and lofty bell tower render it an unmistakable architectural and historic landmark. Its amazing proportion of young Catholics as members—surely the envy of any parish—reflects the sheer concentration within a few blocks of rising professionals drawn by Minneapolis' employment opportunities in the managerial and technical sectors. The nearby Laurel Village apartments symbolize the proximity that makes going to church an easy walk for many. Yet it is common knowledge that location alone will not guarantee a thriving church for younger or older members. Something there must draw them.

As my plane rose and headed southwest, I thought of my interview with Chris Deets, chair of the Creative Stewardship Committee. He is typical of the young professionals who lend their talents to the Basilica. When I asked what drew him to the parish and kept him here for the last five years, he explained:

When I came here, the associate pastor at the time, Father Dale Korogi, had a very warm, inviting, and open air about him. He made you feel like you were a guest in his home. Once I got involved in the work here, I was attracted by how seriously they take spirituality and your faith. They mix that with contemporary fun and sensibilities and dialogue and activities. But they don't give up history and tradition. By tradition I mean the Basilica itself, its liturgy, and the reverence with which they take our faith and communicate it. And still not afraid to have a Block Party with bands. A unique mix. As I started to volunteer here, I started to rediscover my faith. And because the Basilica is so focused on keeping strict attention to the faith and to the symbolism and tradition, they have something that gets lost in our culture. You know, we constantly tear down old buildings and start something new; we're a culture of change. But things that are practiced here haven't changed in a thousand years. My fiancée is going to become a Catholic and what I told her was, you have to take Catholicism within the context of your own life, apply it, and translate the teaching into how it can touch your own life and really affect you. Let me put it another way: If you *want* to look at Catholicism as a thousand years of guilt, well, that's one way of looking at it. But another way is, these traditions mean something or else they wouldn't have lasted so long. If you try hard enough and open your mind and your heart, you will find that meaning and it *will* apply to you. It's worked for me and brought me to five years worth of giving to this parish.

Implied in Chris Deets's praise for the Basilica are the elements that make it a showcase for stewardship implementation:

1) *A rector experienced in and committed to promoting stewardship* "in season and out of season," together with a director of Finance and Administration who shares his vision. Both, particularly Father O'Connell, articulate the *theology* of stewardship repeatedly both orally and in writing, for example in articles in *Basilica* magazine. I emphasize *theology* because both men are careful not to reduce stewardship to simply a fund-raising strategy. This approach affects how committee chairs and members approach stewardship, too—with the spiritual vision of stewardship in the forefront. It is this vision that enables the rector to preach directly about financial giving and strategies such as pledging in ways that encourage people to give rather than turn them off.

Finally, he, along with Tom Green, takes pains to let parishioners know how much they do for the Basilica's mission of service to the congregation and to the broader metropolitan community. Stewardship becomes an expression of active and explicit thankfulness from parish leadership that in turn motivates parishioners to further generosity.

2) *Recruitment to committees of skilled professionals,* who bring two kinds of gifts to the table: a creativity that comes through in ways evident in the interview with Chris Deets. Choosing strategies that use modes of expression and particular approaches aimed at younger members and the highly organized and structured approaches to the work of the two stewardship committees—this again reflects the professional work backgrounds of the members. Little time is wasted in abstract discussions; instead, meetings are characterized by a sharp focus on goals and how to achieve them, accentuating the sense that time spent in committee meetings and planning is worthwhile as it bolsters a feeling of solidarity arising from shared tasks.

These two "gifts" are complemented by interactive committee memberships, that is, a representative of one committee sits on another one, facilitating open communication, planning while reducing "turf guarding." Finally and importantly, the rector exercises leadership by way of partnership, listening and accepting suggestions and allowing himself to be overriden by votes, all of which promotes a true spirit of ownership and cohesion among the staff, committee chairs, and members. It also enhances parishioners' willingness to serve: Their contributions are taken seriously.

3) *Development of new-member orientations* that go beyond the traditional welcoming found in many parishes. Inviting new parishioners to dinner or to Sunday brunch creates the sense that they are truly valued and opens them to appeals for financial support, including pledging. Enhanced giving and volunteering from new members attending these events, as reported by Tom Green in the spring of 2000, confirm the wisdom of this approach.

4) *Building on a decades-long tradition of ministry development and service,* the Basilica has not hesitated to install full-time, paid positions for directors. Interviews with Sue Hayes and Janice Andersen demonstrate the value of this strategy, since it motivates those hired to give fully of their talents and to seek new ways of reaching out to those they serve. From this willingness to consider new ideas there emerge bold and "risky" innovations, such as the highly successful annual Block Party.

To return to a theme of this book, the Basilica of Saint Mary demonstrates both types of social capital, *bridging* and *bonding*. Bridging is illustrated by the bringing together of generations in the work of ministry and in the ecumenical character of outreach projects such as the Jeremiah Program. Bonding social capital is abundantly evident in the sense of enthusiastic identification with fellow parishioners serving in ministerial capacities.

The "Basilica team" is not just a rhetorical flourish. As Robert Putnam points out in *Bowling Alone: The Collapse and Revival of American Community,* "Those of us who belong to formal and informal networks are more likely to give our time and money to good causes than those of us who are isolated socially."[5] And while Putnam is certainly correct in asserting that social ties are as important as religious beliefs in accounting for volunteering,[6] respect is due to the power of stewardship theology, once internalized, to lend a motivational belief dynamic that

---

[5] Robert D. Putnam, *Bowling Alone: The Collapse and Revival of American Community* (New York: Simon and Schuster, 2000) 117.

[6] Ibid., 67.

can sustain and build up within a congregation over time the willingness to sacrifice for common goals seen as worthwhile.

In no way can this dynamic or spirit be achieved in just a year or two, as the Basilica's struggle, particularly with stewardship giving, readily illustrates. Sustained, creative effort over time, however, can indeed bestow on parishioners, in Father O'Connell's words, "the experience of deeper faith that comes from making a sacrificial commitment of their precious resources of time and money."[7]

[7] Michael J. O'Connell, "Generosity Reflects Faith in God," *Basilica* (Autumn 1996) 4.

Chapter 8

Cherishing and Fostering the Gifts of All

Whether adopting a stewardship approach for the first time or renewing it later, pastors, parish staffs, and committee members usually welcome all the help they can get. Diocesan support programs step in to fill this need, recognizing the severe time constraints on pastors and parish staff. Such programs are, in my view, underrecognized. I have chosen two I consider outstanding for the stewardship development and renewal programs they offer. They are scarcely the only dioceses deserving of commendation. We have seen the key role played by the Development and Stewardship Office of the Diocese of Oakland in helping the Corpus Christi Parish begin their program. I have chosen programs of the Archdioceses of St. Louis and Seattle largely because they are among the oldest and most developed. They demonstrate that stewardship need lose none of its "charismatic" character by being promoted from within a top-level bureaucratic structure. Directed by staffs truly convinced of and committed to the spread of stewardship ideals and practices, these offices constitute a godsend to pastors and parish councils or commissions willing to give stewardship a try and welcoming help in getting started or in renewing a program that needs a lift. We have already seen two parishes—Corpus Christi and St. Peter's—that profited greatly from just this kind of diocesan impetus.

The Archdiocese of St. Louis: A Pioneer Program

The Gateway City is a good place to begin. After all, it was here that the National Council for Diocesan Support Programs came into being in 1962 under the patronage of Cardinal Joseph Ritter. Father Paul Kaletta of the archdiocese became the Council's first director. In 1968 it was renamed the National (and later International) Catholic Stewardship Council, moving its office to Washington. But the Archdiocese of St. Louis continued to have an active Office of Stewardship. In 1986 the Office of Stewardship and Development (OSD) began to offer support programs to help initiate and maintain a stewardship approach in parishes. Frank Cognata, Jr., current chief development officer, served on the board of the National Catholic Stewardship Council and is an unflagging supporter of educational programs like those developed by OSD. In fact, the educational materials developed by Cognata's office have been recognized for excellence by the current International Catholic Stewardship Council. Susan Erschen currently serves as the director of Stewardship Education within OSD.

Like many dioceses, the Archdiocese of St. Louis incorporated stewardship within a fully developed "Strategic Pastoral Plan: 1999–2002," which states: "The purpose of our Strategic Pastoral Planning is to enhance the vitality of the Church of the Archdiocese of St. Louis by providing a focus for our human and material resources according to selected priorities consistent with the stated vision of our Archbishop."[1]

The Strategic Plan outlines five goals in the following order: (1) to foster conversion through prayer and the sacraments; (2) to proclaim Jesus Christ in Word and Action (evangelization); (3) to renew our commitment to Catholic education in all its forms; (4) to serve those in need; (5) to be responsible stewards of God's gifts to us.[2]

Among the five priorities listed under the fifth goal, "to be responsible stewards," are "to teach stewardship as a way of life among all people of the Archdiocese," and "to practice stewardship beyond the limits of parishes and agencies." Implicit in the first priority, of course, is that OSD is to continue its long-standing mission of assisting parishes in adopting a stewardship approach. In the second priority, OSD explicitly commends parishes initiating

[1] Archdiocese of St. Louis, *Strategic Pastoral Plan: 1999–2002* (St. Louis: The Catholic Center, 1999) iv.
   [2] Ibid.

a time and talent exchange process in which parishes are able to share resources to meet needs, collaborat[ing] with the regional director of volunteers for Catholic Charities to identify ways of parishes to share gifts with charitable organizations, and produc[ing] a rough draft, along with Catholic Charities, of a Directory for Volunteer Opportunities within the Archdiocese.

After many years of developing and administering a successful program that has reached more than two hundred parishes in the archdiocese, OSD drew on this experience in 2000 to codify its approach and procedures in a comprehensive fashion. *A Guide to Conducting Stewardship Education in the Parish* is a model document of 170 pages. An overview of its major sections conveys a sense of the detailed thoroughness of the *Guide:*

AN INTRODUCTION TO STEWARDSHIP

After a definition of the term, answers are posed to a series of questions: How does stewardship differ from fund-raising? Why should we teach it? Must it be taught every year? Will it really differ from fund-raising? Will it really work? What are its benefits? There follow several pages of scriptural references to stewardship from both the Old and New Testaments, including Gospel "stewardship stories." The bishops' letter on stewardship is reviewed, followed by a history of stewardship in the archdiocese and how it fits into the archdiocesan Strategic Plan. The last section outlines "Important Steps to Success": establishing a full stewardship committee; recognizing that stewardship is not only about money; thinking carefully about who your lay witness speakers will be; preparing all parish organizations to embrace stewardship; continuously educating yourself regarding successful stewardship; modeling good stewardship.

THE STEWARDSHIP CALENDAR

"The Basic Calendar" following demonstrates the detail with which OSD pursues its educational mission. Five subsequent calendar pages are devoted to "A Typical Fall Renewal Program," furthering OSD's strategy of detailed suggestions on how to proceed.

The Basic Calendar

Learning to live as stewards is a lifelong process. You can't put a timeline together for how each of us will respond to God's call to stewardship. The stewardship education program, however, does follow a very simple timetable. No matter what time of the year your parish decides to conduct stewardship education, you will be most successful if you can follow this timetable.

	Mon.	Tues.	Wed.	Thurs.	Fri.	Sat. / Sun.
Week 1	Submit appropriate bulletin insert					**Priest's Talk on Stewardship** Stewardship "Prayers of the Faithful"
Week 2	Submit appropriate bulletin insert					**Lay Witness Pulpit Talk** Distribute time and talent catalogs **Festival of Ministries** Stewardship "Prayers of the Faithful"
Week 3	Submit appropriate bulletin insert Mail personalized letter with brochure and intention card					**Intention Sunday** Intention cards returned in offertory basket Stewardship "Prayers of the Faithful"
Week 4	Submit appropriate bulletin insert Begin recording intention cards Compile telephone follow-up list	Begin telephone follow-up Begin mailing thank you notes	Telephone follow-up	Telephone follow-up		**Second Intention Sunday** Parish provides extra intention cards in church Stewardship "Prayers of the Faithful"
Week 5	Record intention cards	Continue sending thank you notes	Send follow-up letters (optional)			
Week 6	Analyze results of intention cards and submit report and "Thank you" to bulletin					

Reprinted from *A Guide to Conducting Stewardship Education in the Parish,* with permission from the Archdiocese of St. Louis, Office of Stewardship & Development © 2000.

The role of the pastor opens this section: why he must preach steward-ship, and his responsibilities to invite and encourage parishioners "to be partners with him" in the stewardship endeavor. Forming the Stewardship Committee includes responsibilities and qualifications of the chair, secretary and/or bookkeeper, the time and talent chair, lay witness speakers, and a telephone committee chair. How important the document views this role is clear from the opening paragraph:

> One of the most critical, and sometimes unappreciated, roles on the stewardship team is that of the parish secretary. [He or she] is ultimately responsible for making the connection with the parish-ioners both *when they are asked to give* their gifts of time, talent and treasure and *after they have offered* to give their time, talent and treasure. The care and concern with which the secretary (and/or bookkeeper) completes the stewardship tasks could have a tremen-dous impact on the overall success of the stewardship educational efforts in the parish. For this reason it is important to include the secretary in all aspects of the stewardship process (emphasis in the original).

In fact, this section flatly makes the following recommendation:

> . . . *it is important that [this person] be a part of the stewardship com-mittee and not just someone who receives orders after all the decisions are made.* If parish secretaries are part of the team they can often add valuable insights into the operation of the parish and the best way to achieve a goal (emphasis in the original).

How to conduct a successful Stewardship Evening is outlined in detail: who should be invited, a suggested letter of invitation from the pastor and a bulletin insert, and a sample agenda for the evening.

The "nuts and bolts" are spelled out in no uncertain terms in this lengthiest of all the sections. Basic educational materials such as a brochure, the pastor's letter, and the intention card are spelled out, as are procedures for pulpit talks. How to devise a Time and Talent catalog and plan a Festival of Ministries follows. Incorporating stewardship into the liturgy receives attention. Thank-you notes, telephone follow-ups, and even a suggested "last chance follow-up letter" conclude this section.

Reaping the Benefits of Your Annual Stewardship Program

This section emphasizes how critical it is to contact and welcome every new member and follow up on their offers of time and talent. Again, details are spelled out: nametags, a "buddy system" to pair newcomers with a parish member, suggestions for terms of commitment, new ways to use volunteers (from parish clean-up day to garden club to unemployed support group and many more), ideas for involving older and homebound parishioners. Involving young adults receives several pages of attention, deservedly so since many parishes find them to be the "missing group" in the parish. The stewardship of treasure is also covered here: sample pledge reminder letters, giving-guide cards, suggested steps upon completion of the pledge phase. Evaluation occupies the final three pages—number of cards returned, percentage of people who participated by returning their card, and also the percentage of parishioners who pledged.

Stewardship All Year

How to use a Stewardship Committee all year opens this section: Are stewardship prayers and bulletin inserts used year round? Working with the school principal to initiate children's stewardship, working with parish organizations to help them utilize new volunteers, and working with the parish liturgy coordinator to see that stewardship-related music and prayers of the faithful are among the many suggestions. Other sections discuss a stewardship newsletter, quarterly and annual reports, ideas for banners, signs, and bulletin boards, buttons, balloons, and giveaways.

Eucharistic adoration is given strong endorsement, as is welcoming new parishioners—a section occupying five full pages. The concluding section, "Spiritual Enrichment for Your Committee," discusses retreats, reflecting on and studying stewardship together and praying for guidance, a faith-and-idea-sharing event with another Stewardship Committee, and "some steps you should follow in planning any spiritual enrichment program."

Attachments include a resource directory listing various archdiocesan offices and their phone numbers, email addresses and/or Web sites, a directory of parishes in the archdiocese actively involved in stewardship, a list of stewardship bulletin reflections, and suggested prayers of the faithful and pulpit announcements.

It is possible that no diocese in the United States has put forth a more painstakingly thorough guide to the implementation, renewal, and maintenance of stewardship. And little wonder that over two hundred parishes within the archdiocese have either initiated or renewed stewardship programs. This is truly an outstanding diocesan educational enterprise. Besides the *Guide,* a quarterly newsletter called *Stewardship Alive!* is sent to all parishes; it contains stewardship inserts for the parish Sunday bulletin, prayers of the faithful, and ideas borrowed from parishes, for example, on conducting a Festival of Ministries. Teaching stewardship to children receives special emphasis, exemplified in another quarterly newsletter, *Stewardship Seeds,* begun in the spring of 2000. Offering stewardship ideas that can be implemented in the classroom, such as artwork for bulletin boards, classroom activities for children's liturgies, and stewardship stories and prayers, this newsletter also provides a column for parents on ways to teach stewardship to their children.

Finally, in a conversation with director Sue Erschen, I asked about the reasons for parishes "wearing down" or "becoming stale" in stewardship endeavors. Her reflections are most instructive:

> I must stress that our renewal programs are not used in places where stewardship has broken down or gotten stale. Our renewal programs are recommended every year in every parish that has begun the stewardship process by using our initial program. Each year we develop new renewal materials. The idea is that every year parishioners are asked to renew and deepen their commitment to stewardship. Stewardship dies out, breaks down, or gets stale in a parish precisely because they do not renew the message every year. I often tell parishes, when they debate whether or not to do renewal, that as Christians we need to constantly be reminded of all the dimensions of our faith. We don't observe Lent or Christmas or Easter just once and say, "Well now, everyone should remember that for the rest of their lives." We shouldn't figure we can just teach stewardship once either. As an individual's faith grows and deepens, he or she will understand and respond to the stewardship message differently throughout life. Thus we need to renew the commitment annually.

Sue further reflected on why parishes decide not to renew stewardship:

> The pastor [is] not very committed to it in the first place; a new
> pastor is not interested; the Stewardship Committee falls apart and
> no one else wants to pick it up (if only one person assumes respon-
> sibility, it is all too easy for that person to burn out); parishes [that]
> demand quick and easy results and are unwilling to invest the time
> to see stewardship grow; or gifts of money are the primary reason
> for adopting stewardship, resulting in parishioners feeling "all
> they want is my money."

The Archdiocese of St. Louis exemplifies how well supported diocesan programs can both serve to get stewardship started within parishes
and assist parish personnel to keep its spirit alive year after year. Creative initiatives come forth regularly from OSD, so that nothing becomes
a stale formula that reduces stewardship to a lifeless routine. Good
listening to pastors and Stewardship Committees also plays a big role
in OSD's responsiveness. Results speak for themselves: Parishes adopting the first-year program experience a 19.4 percent average increase in
weekly contributions. For the renewal program, the average increase is
10.4 percent. All parishes experience a notable increase in volunteers
for organizations and ministries.

The Archdiocese of Seattle:
Blending Sacrificial Giving with Stewardship

Seattle's archbishops and development staffs have long supported
sacrificial giving as a motivational concept, particularly for the stewardship of treasure. Msgr. Joseph Champlin's development of sacrificial
giving as a motivational perspective has influenced thousands of
Catholic clergy and laity in the United States.[3] In fact, Scott Bader's title
in the archdiocese is director of Sacrificial Giving and Parish Development. Almost 90 percent of parishes in the archdiocese have adopted
this concept. As Bader wrote to me,

---

[3] Through his frequent appearances as a speaker and through his book *Sharing
Treasure, Time and Talent: A Parish Manual for Sacrificial Giving or Tithing* (Collegeville,
Minn.: The Liturgical Press, 1982), Msgr. Joseph M. Champlin has influenced
numerous parishes to adopt this perspective.

. . . this high percentage fluctuates a little, as some parishes break off each year to do a capital campaign that may or may not incorporate the spirit of stewardship and sacrificial giving, and some come back each year after a capital campaign. Some parishes begin with a pastor change. A little over 80 percent of our parishes do our program entirely (at least in terms of ordering materials).

What, then, is the ethos behind this concept? Scott Bader's office has spelled it out quite eloquently in a small brochure entitled "New at This," which is part of a packet of materials made available to parishes:

> Sacrificial giving is one way we have of walking in the footsteps of Our Lord, who sacrificed everything so that we might have life. We give up something of ourselves so that life can flourish. When we give that way we are changed. When giving becomes sacrificial giving, it focuses our attention on the true source of our security. When we give away something we think we need to survive, we are saying that money won't take care of us, possessions won't save us. Sacrificial giving bears witness to the reality that God alone will make us safe. Recognizing that reality and living it out constitute a tremendous change in our lives. And this can make an equally tremendous difference to the lives of others. The sacrifice we make by doing without some portion of our substance is just that: doing without so that life for others may flourish.

The Giving of Treasure—The "Sacrificial Giving Campaign" proceeds in three phases for a parish agreeing to participate:

Pre-Campaign Preparation

September or early October is suggested as the best time to deliver an annual financial report to the parish, set in a broader context of parish life and activities. Each donor is to be mailed a record of his or her gifts through that quarter with a personalized thank-you letter from the pastor or pastoral life director, together with a quarterly financial report. The parish bulletin notes any accomplishments due to the financial generosity of parishioners, such as paying off a debt, aiding the poor, completing a repair.

The pastor is urged to share any experiences related by parishioners because they got involved in sacrificial giving. Specific formats for a parish annual report, a financial report, and a statement of parish goals and objectives are included. Detailed directions follow for setting up a

Sacrificial Giving Committee composed of parishioners who are proven givers of time, talent, and treasure. They should be good communicators, possessing both written and verbal skills, as well as visionaries with a sense of direction for the parish and the Church; they should also be comfortable talking about money and willing to model accountability in reporting back to parishioners.

Goal-setting for commitment cards comes next: 10 percent more than the number returned last year *or* 50 percent of parish households (a fast-growing parish might want to set the goal even higher). High expectations, pastors are reminded, motivate parishioners to increase their pledges or begin a commitment for the first time. These expectations also motivate the parish staff to work toward adopted goals.

The pre-campaign preparation phase closes by suggesting that the parish model sacrificial giving by donating a percentage of parish income to programs or charities at local, regional, national, and international levels. "Parishes that have chosen to do this have found that their own needs are in better perspective." A parish might start by setting aside 1 or 2 percent of income and gradually increase that percentage over time. A Challenge Grant Option is also proposed. The parish contacts a parishioner who might be willing to give a "significant donation" on condition that the parish meet its sacrificial giving goals. Or it simply sets and publicizes a goal, which might be a certain number of commitment cards or a specific total pledged.

PRESENTING THE PROGRAM

Seattle's directives for implementing sacrificial giving are set forth in the same encouraging detail we see in the St. Louis Archdiocesan program. A parish knows exactly how to go about this. November is the suggested month for the actual appeal. Parishioners are alerted ahead of time to the forthcoming appeal. Posters, a variety of media, mailings, bulletin and pulpit announcements—all are to be focused on promoting the onset of sacrificial giving. Personalized letters and mailing labels are recommended ("avoid using window envelopes: this signifies junk mail to many people"). Using first-class postage will emphasize the importance of the contents. Model letters are included in the packet—and not just one version. Several campaign, thank-you, and follow-up letter formats are offered for the pastor or pastoral life director. A remarkable extension of helpfulness to parishioners is an

Other Half Worksheet, which could easily serve as a model for parishes anywhere (see next page). Also given is the page listing suggested announcements.

The packet conveys admirably the entire November appeal sequence from the initial announcement through the pastor's thank-you at the end of the month. "Witness Talks" occupies several pages: selection and recruitment; ensuring effectiveness of the presentations, that is, scheduling them immediately after the homily, not at the end of Mass; and walking the congregation through filling out the commitment card right after the witness presentation. A Witnessing Packet includes a training videotape and a host of suggestions for the talk itself. Some examples: *do* refer to your own giving experiences in telling what sacrificial giving means to you; *do* emphasize the joy that comes to those who give God their "first shares"; *don't* use "bargaining language," such as "When I gave this much, this is what God did for me" (or for us); *don't* emphasize church needs or budgets; *don't* talk about sacrificial giving as an obligation.

I add the following examples from the explanations of these *dos* and *don'ts* because they admirably set forth the spirit of sacrificial giving that informs the entire program:

> People relate far more readily to God's blessings than to a parish budget. When motivated to give out of gratitude and justice, they begin to give the gift God really wants—themselves. In doing so, they experience joy. Emphasizing the personal need of each individual to give eliminates arguments. The need is universal. Suggesting that sacrificial giving is an obligation invites challenges we can never answer. Making it voluntary places it where it belongs: It is one of the many things generous Catholics do—not out of law but out of love.

Again the point is brought home to each giver that sacrificial giving is a need everyone has. It is the way one gives of himself or herself to God. The following is the conclusion of an example of a lay witness (three examples are given in the diocesan material), inspiring words that might be heard in virtually any stewardship parish across the country:

> Before I began tithing, for a long time I had struggled with tight-fistedness—a stinginess and hardness of heart, with the result that although I was able to give some of my time once in a while for a good cause, I could not seem to open up that fist and give of my

Other Half Worksheet

A worksheet to help you plan and budget your giving to charity.

All of us receive requests from many charities throughout the year—and sometimes our response is one of weariness or anxiety. Why me? My resources are limited? How can I take care of them all? But these various requests present the opportunity to plan our giving—to share the blessings God has given us, and experience the joy of sharing.

<u>We are asked to split our gift in half—
one half to the parish, and the other half to charities of our choice.</u>

Some Charities to Consider for the 'Other Half'

<u>Local Assistance for the Poor and Needy</u>
St. Vincent De Paul $_____

Catholic Community Services (December) $_____
    provides social services support to families throughout Washington

<u>Catholic Schools</u> $_____
    elementary school and high school fund drives

Annual Catholic Appeal (May) $_____
    funds a wide range of archdiocesan programs and services

Other $_____

<u>Special National and International Church Collections</u>
Bishops Overseas Aid Appeal (March) $_____
    supports Catholic Relief Services overseas

Peter's Pence (June) $_____
    provides funds for ministries especially overseen by the Holy Father

Build Hope (September) $_____
    addresses root causes of poverty in our county and funds evangelization

Mission Sunday (October) $_____
    supports Catholic missionary efforts throughout the world

<u>Other Charities</u>

_____ $_____

_____ $_____

Announcements

It is important to keep focusing the attention of the parishioners on Sacrificial Giving throughout the campaign. There is no telling how subtle reminders from the pulpit and bulletin might affect the success of the Sacrificial Giving program—they are low cost media.

Feel free to modify the bulletin and pulpit announcements to fit your parish's own needs and circumstances.

In-Church Announcements

#1   FIRST WEEKEND IN NOVEMBER:

This week you will be receiving a very important mailing about Sacrificial Giving. I ask that you spend a few minutes during the next week to read this material carefully and reflect upon God's blessings prayerfully. This will help all of us to be ready for the presentation we will hear about Sacrificial Giving next weekend.

#2   SECOND WEEKEND IN NOVEMBER:

Thanks to those of you who have already returned your Sacrificial Giving Commitment Card. I ask everyone else to reflect upon the witness presentation you have heard today and prayerfully evaluate your giving to the parish and community. Please also take some time to read over the insert in today's bulletin about Sacrificial Giving. The joy of giving back to God's community is great. We ask that all our parishioners return their Commitment Card next weekend in the collection basket.

#3   THIRD WEEKEND IN NOVEMBER:

If you have not already done so, please bring your Sacrificial Giving Commitment Card with you to Mass next weekend or return it to the parish by mail. We will be mailing another Commitment Card to those who have not yet responded. It is important for all of us to return a Commitment Card so we can meet our parish goal.

#4   FOURTH WEEKEND IN NOVEMBER:

Our Sacrificial Giving campaign is coming to a close. On behalf of our parish, I want to thank all of you who have responded and returned a Sacrificial Giving Commitment Card. Your commitment will enable us not only to continue our work for God's people, but hopefully will also enable us to expand our efforts to carry out Christ's mission through our parish's efforts.

May the generous blessings of God's Spirit continue to nourish you in the days to come, and may the joy of giving be yours.

Reprinted from the Sacrificial Giving Binder of the Archdiocese of Seattle with permission from the Archdiocese of Seattle, Office of Sacrificial Giving and Parish Development.

money with the same good spirit. Every so-called gift was given with a cold, calculated entry into an imaginary ledger where I balanced "Sacrifices Made" with "Rewards Expected." A ledger of financial indulgences, so to speak. But as I embarked on this adventure of sacrificial giving, dedicating the first part of my income to the Lord, I immediately sensed a loosening of the grip, and as my fist unclenched and as I let go of my dependency on material possessions and put my trust in God's Providence, my life has been blessed with a harmony and radiance that it never had before. My faith is on firmer ground. My heart's in the right place. It really is true, you know, "Where your treasure is, there also will be your heart." And through the giving I felt a sense of sharing in the work that is being done, the good work of the Lord that's being done through my gifts. And because the giving has been cheerful, and not grudging or calculated, it's been fun. And therein lies the joy. I invite you to come—share this joy.

Completed commitment cards are to be presented at Mass along with the gifts as part of the offertory. As the gifts come forward, the presider is to receive the baskets of contributions and commitment cards, placing them in front of (but not on) the altar. "This serves to dramatize the spiritual dimensions of Sacrificial Giving." Furthermore, the pastor or pastoral life director is to ask for the commitment card, an act deemed "extremely critical to the entire campaign." Not doing so risks wasting "most all of the effort made to get . . . parishioners to give." A high percentage of those present at Mass will not have remembered to bring the card they received in the mail. "Asking" in church and giving people ample time to fill out the cards results in "about half of all cards" coming from the pews, a strategy much more successful than expecting all cards to be returned by mail.

Post-Campaign Pursuits

Directions for conducting telephone follow-ups ("Pick volunteers who like dealing with people") is followed by a suggested script for the calls, with answers to questions or statements often encountered:

"Why should I make a written pledge?"
"We're having financial difficulties right now."
"How much should I (we) pledge?"
"What about all the people in my parish who give nothing at all?"

Tips are given for quarterly report mailings, the use of envelopes and envelope artwork, and finally a list of "other options for year-round stewardship." Among these options are youth and children's stewardship; a half-day workshop on stewardship for all parish leaders; a six-week RENEW-style small study group on the bishops' pastoral letter on stewardship, *Stewardship: A Disciple's Response,* emphasizing social justice and environmental concerns.

Scott Bader's office also offers a collection of materials expanding on the liturgical incorporation of sacrificial giving, scriptural texts for announcements or talks, parables of Jesus dealing with money and possessions, and extended theological reflections on sacrificial giving by Father Michael B. Raschko of the archdiocese, currently on the faculty of the Institute of Theological Studies at Seattle University. Bibliographies of written resource materials and videotapes relating to sacrificial giving and to stewardship are also available.

Giving of Time and Talent

As Scott Bader pointed out to me, parishes request time and talent materials somewhat less often than those on sacrificial giving. His office, however, is prepared with *Sharing Our Gifts: Time and Talent Manual.* Following a summary of the U.S. bishops' *Stewardship: A Disciple's Response,* the manual presents an outline for a time and talent campaign. Early summer is suggested for initial planning. A key component is a Ministry Guide listing all the ministries and services in the parish, together with the name and phone number of a contact person for each ministry or service.

In September parishioners are alerted through announcements that they will receive materials concerning the stewardship of time and talent. Early that month a Ministry Fair is suggested for information only (no sign-ups). Parishioners can simply explore these displays while being informed of a ministry-involvement survey to be distributed in the pews. As with sacrificial giving, the pastor leads the congregation in filling out the survey form. The next, and critical, element is to immediately contact parishioners who have returned the survey form.

Involved parishioners are urged to set up a Parish Development Program. Among the responsibilities of parish leaders in this program is an annual report that can take the form of the guide or brochure mentioned above, listing all ministries with a contact person and phone number. A yearly events calendar may be attached. Mailing this report to all registered households is strongly recommended.

The *Sharing Our Gifts: Time and Talent Manual* underlines the importance of a Ministry Fair, "an extravaganza in which all ministries, programs, services, and activities are showcased at one time, each having their own table, booth or space." The manual continues:

> This is an educational event in which parishioners are able to meet people and gather information about the various ministries within the parish, enabling them to make a better decision as they choose where to serve. *No solicitation is allowed.* This event allows parishioners to ask questions, and also brings them to a greater awareness of all the opportunities the parish has to offer [emphasis in the original].

The manual then suggests specific bulletin and pulpit announcements, with a recommended schedule for mailings and letters to parishioners who return a card. A formal "Commissioning Ceremony for Ministries" for new participants is followed by guidelines for an appreciation dinner honoring those who already give of their time and talent. Awards may be given to those who are leaving a ministry.

Once again, St. Louis and Seattle are not the only dioceses offering commendable stewardship assistance to parishes. They are simply excellent examples of such programs. An unspoken premise of these efforts, with all their detailed directions and suggestions, is that pastors are more than busy enough with what parish leadership requires of them, a situation becoming all the more acute because of the priest shortage. Offering detailed assistance obviously makes it easier for pastors to say yes to initiating a plan and provides a road map for the parish staff and council leaders, who play such key roles in implementing the program.

Directors like Susan Erschen in St. Louis and Scott Bader in Seattle are fully aware that parishes may not "buy into" everything offered. They often pick and choose from materials offered, declining some elements while accepting others. Some parishes develop "home grown" approaches. Diocesan directors expect adaptation, and they welcome feedback. Both diocesan programs have advisory councils of active parish personnel that review what works and what does not, resulting in a cybernetic model in which feedback helps directors streamline and modify programs.

Parishes benefit in every way. By working with an Archdiocesan Office of Stewardship, individual parishes can avoid duplication of effort. Instead of having to research stewardship educational options and design their own materials, parishes can rely on the knowledge and expertise of archdiocesan personnel, who are committed to researching and offering the best stewardship information possible.

Working through a diocesan office, parishes profit from the experiences of other parishes not only within their own diocese but across the nation, since diocesan offices are more likely to be aware of local, national, and international trends and related Church teachings. By using prepared resources within their own diocese, parishes are spared the time and expense of either preparing their own materials or turning to for-profit suppliers. In a word, these offices form an excellent example of institutional linkages that facilitate work "on the front line."

Other benefits are less obvious, residing in the domain that sociologists call "latent functions." Veteran pastors have been known to express serious misgivings (putting it mildly for some!) about diocesan offices ("those bureaucrats downtown"). A few go even further with complaints that "all they do is take from us" (diocesan assessments). Diocesan personnel are well aware of these negative views. Thus a program like this that translates into concrete and welcome services for pastors also helps to improve relationships between dioceses and parishes.

The success of the treasure aspect of stewardship and sacrificial giving patently creates a win/win situation by enhancing revenues at both parish and diocesan levels, and this success more than repays the time and expense to the diocese of maintaining stewardship support programs. These programs also provide positions for those well-trained, highly skilled laypersons who believe they are called to serve the Catholic Church and value full-time employment that allows them to do so. As the clergy shortage continues, their services shift from the "helpful" to "invaluable" in carrying out the mission of the Catholic Church in the United States.

Chapter 9

Conclusion:
The Promise of Stewardship

I began this book with a rather dispiriting sociological portrait of American Catholics today. Indifference seems to be growing—their Church seems less central to the lives of Catholics than it was to their parents. A younger generation of Catholics, while not rejecting Catholic identity, is hard to detect on the radar scopes of many, if not most, Catholic parishes. Additional organizational strains stem from Catholics' chronically low giving plus the growing priest shortage. Added together, these factors spell out a religious institution whose overall resource bases are in precarious condition despite the shining examples of individual parishes across the United States.

Against this background comes the challenge of stewardship, an internally generated and sustained movement to motivate Catholics of all ages and backgrounds to be more willing to support their parishes financially and with volunteer service. As we have seen, this movement is undergirded by a Scripture-based theology endorsed and elaborated by the Catholic bishops. It is promoted organizationally by both the International Catholic Stewardship Council (ICSC), mainly through its national and regional conventions, and by individual dioceses through support programs developed to help parishes adopt a stewardship approach to money and ministries. In this context, stewardship assumes the shape of an institutionally supported revitalization movement, not directed "from the Vatican on down" but springing up from *within* the American Catholic Church at three levels: ICSC, the diocese, and the parish.

The timeliness of this movement is evident in the light of research reviewed in the Introduction. In an era of shrinking social capital, as measured by Americans' declining civic participation and increasing individualism, stewardship issues a call to Catholic parishioners to serve within their parishes and to develop new forms of ministry serving both parishioners and those outside parish borders. In doing so, stewardship becomes a force moving Catholic parishes from "Houses of Worship" to centers of true community formation and outreach, particularly exemplified by "advanced" stewardship parishes like St. John the Baptist in Covington, Washington, and the Basilica of Saint Mary in Minneapolis.

By motivating parish members to work together in various forms of service, a stewardship approach generates both bonding and bridging social capital: It helps parishioners form working alliances and friendships in the process of shared ministry activity (bonding) and also reaches out to others with whom they would ordinarily have little contact (bridging), whether it be low-income mothers and their children in the Jeremiah Program in Minneapolis or inner-city residents through St. Marcelline's neighborhood revitalization project in Chicago's Lawndale area. Each parish in this book gives evidence of lively generation of both kinds of social capital. In this sense, stewardship responds to a vital need not just within the American Catholic Church but within American society itself.

Also timely is the role of stewardship in that most challenging of pastoral responsibilities: asking for money. Robert Wuthnow's research points squarely to the forms of ambivalence and denial characterizing Americans' attitude toward money. Here the stewardship approach can promise no instant results. If anything is clear from the case studies, it is that success in the treasure dimension of stewardship almost always comes more slowly than success in the time and talent dimensions. The more successful parishes—St. Gerard Majella, St. John the Baptist, the Basilica of Saint Mary among them—are relatively long-term practitioners of stewardship. To be sure, location in a diocese sponsoring a stewardship support program, such as Seattle or St. Louis, certainly helps; these programs can jump-start a stewardship program, but steady, long-term gains in regular giving require the continuous, creative promotion of stewardship.

This qualified optimism runs counter to seriously considered misgivings about stewardship. Robert Wuthnow dedicates Chapter 8, "The Demise of Stewardship," in *The Crisis in the Churches: Spiritual Malaise,*

Fiscal Woe, to these misgivings, referring mainly, though not exclusively, to American Protestant Churches. He elaborates on several "Difficulties with the Message,"[1] making four key points:

1. *Stewardship is an important teaching but is difficult to communicate* because it runs directly counter to parishioners' self-interest. The latter "encourages us to think in relativistic, calculating, situational terms, whereas many pastors regard stewardship as an absolute, morally binding obligation. . . . The more pervasive problem may be that self-interest encourages us to think more in terms of choice, freedom, options, and lifestyles than in terms of responsibilities . . . choosing the lifestyle that makes us happiest."[2]

2. *Pastors often assume "a priestly role" in preaching stewardship,* focusing on support for the church and its ministries. Downplayed is the "prophetic role" of speaking out against "self-interest . . . working too hard, in favor of using one's talents wisely at the office, and on behalf of the environment."[3] The meaning of stewardship is thus confined mainly to serving on church committees, projects, etc.

3. *Clergy continue to "have trouble speaking clearly about stewardship* in relation to work and money . . . [they] tie themselves in knots trying to explain how people should be good stewards at work."[4] Some pastors support parishioners' making all the money they can but urge them to use it wisely. Church members in the pews, however, may also suspect that "God's servants have a special place in their heart for the rich."[5] Stewardship thus conveyed indeed suggests that people are caretakers of what God has given. Yet this general message tends to leave people directionless: "Contemporary caretakers do not check in with the boss very often or receive very explicit instructions on what to do. Rather, they are like good business managers: Not knowing exactly what the owner expects, they simply try to do what's good for the company."[6]

Wuthnow's suggestions for a more authentic stewardship reflect many of the "lessons" or principles apparent in the case studies we

---

[1] Robert Wuthnow, *The Crisis in the Churches: Spiritual Malaise, Fiscal Woe* (New York: Oxford University Press, 1997) 126.

[2] Ibid., 127.

[3] Ibid., 128.

[4] Ibid., 130.

[5] Ibid., 133.

[6] Ibid., 134.

have seen: Churches must continue to emphasize the *theological* significance of stewardship, to call for a *balance* in people's lives in the areas of worship, work, rest, and play. Stewardship needs to challenge "the prevailing ideology of self-interest." It must help members see that they are stewards in the broad range of their lives and that churches alone cannot do God's work. Finally, churches must help people rediscover the value of rituals in their daily lives: "One man told us he lights a candle every day for a few minutes in his office as a reminder that everything is God's and a part of the spirit of God. A Methodist pastor told us she likes to dig in the dirt with her daughter and talk about how God is present in her garden."[7]

4. *Churches must be enablers*, supporting parishioners in efforts to live their lives responsibly, in protecting the environment, and in using resources for the benefit of others: "Pastoral counseling, training in financial management, and opportunities to serve the needy are among the ways in which churches can turn talk about stewardship into action. Such activities can be performed in cooperation with other churches and with non-religious agencies in the community and in the workplace."[8]

The churches portrayed in this volume have done much to address "difficulties with the message" and to implement stewardship in ways advocated by Wuthnow. One advantage accruing to Catholic churches is that they come new to stewardship. Not only have they learned a good deal from their Protestant neighbors, clergy and lay, but as newcomers Catholic pastors and "faithful" do not, by and large, experience the notion of stewardship as old hat, and thus as a hoary metaphor devoid of vital relevance to their lives. A major challenge is to *maintain* stewardship as a vital concept and a meaningful, productive program in decades to come. Some major findings, then, that touch on solutions to the problems sketched above are the following.

The Pastor's Genuine, Personal Conversion to Stewardship

We read in the pastors' own accounts, strikingly illustrated at St. Gerard Majella, Corpus Christi, St. John the Baptist, and the Basilica of Saint Mary, but truly present in all the parishes, the centrality of the

[7] Ibid., 138.
[8] Ibid.

pastor's role in, and commitment to, carrying stewardship ideals forward, sustaining them year after year. The pastor's dedication to proportionate giving and pledging in his own life serves as an inspirational beacon to the staff and parishioners (see St. Gerard Majella Parish, Chapter 5). This impact is enhanced if the pastor articulates "in season and out of season" a vision of where he would like to see the parish go under stewardship and how to get there. Perhaps above all, his stewardship conversion enables him to talk frankly and fearlessly about money, directly addressing the "blockage" analyzed in the Wuthnow research. Examples are abundant in the sermons quoted in this volume. If this vision and spirit of forthright addressing of finances are accompanied by a willingness to adopt a partnership stance toward the staff and lay leadership in parish governance (St. John the Baptist Parish, Chapter 6), the pastor's leadership can truly inspire and motivate parishioners to attain new levels of generosity, particularly if expectations are spelled out clearly, as in the "Grow One" approach.

A key to the pastor's conversion and dedication to stewardship ideals is his exposure to the stewardship paradigm at a national or regional convention or through attendance at diocesan-sponsored stewardship events such as "Stewardship Evenings." There is no substitute for such personal contact. Stewardship cannot be delegated just to the parish staff: "If we send Joe, Julie, and Art to the convention, they'll come back and show us all how to do it." The case studies in this volume are unanimous on this point: The pastor's convictions, gained through personal and prayerful involvement, are utterly essential to effective stewardship. Most pastors understand this. They are indeed visible at national and regional conventions leading delegations from their parishes.

There Is No Such Thing as a Stewardship "Cookie-Cutter Recipe" that Fits All Churches

Once again, the stewardship stories in this volume demonstrate how distinctive parishes are from one another in history, demographics, personnel, and membership. Thoughtful adaptation is always called for, as in the case of St. Peter Parish in Kirkwood, Missouri (Chapter 2). The transition from a parish-supported school to one that is tuition-supported school called for a sensitive approach to stewardship of treasure. As diocesan stewardship directors freely admit, parishes adapt diocesan programs, tailoring them to their own needs and situations as they perceive them. A tremendous advantage, of course, accrues to a parish *beginning* with a stewardship approach (St. John the Baptist, Chapter 6).

Creation of a Stewardship Committee Is Vital to Program Success

Stewardship will not work if it is delivered as an "add-on" to the responsibilities of the Pastoral Council or the Finance Commission. The Basilica of Saint Mary (Chapter 7) is but one example of the vital role of a Stewardship Committee in setting and maintaining a *vision* for the parish community, detailing over time what is to be accomplished and how to promote understanding and acceptance of stewardship ideals among parish members. These are fully engaging challenges for members of a Stewardship Committee, calling on the creative energies of all participants to create colorful and attention-getting ways of keeping stewardship ideals before the congregation—posters, music, ministry fairs, and even processions (see Corpus Christi Parish, Chapter 1), as well as finding energetic ways to integrate stewardship themes into the liturgy and the Sunday bulletin.

The Stewardship Committee is a resource for ideas promoting stewardship among children, indeed among all age groups. The range of possibilities suggesting the wisdom of inclusivity in committee membership is virtually infinite. Why not teen representatives suggesting how to reach their peers? Does the committee represent, to some degree at least, the ethnic/cultural makeup of the parish? Why not include the parish secretary as an ex-officio member (who knows better how to gauge parishioner reaction to a proposed course of action?). Liaison with other parish committees or commissions can be accomplished through designation of members who regularly attend meetings of the Pastoral Council and the Finance Commission, and whose delegates attend meetings of the Stewardship Committee.

Integration of Stewardship Themes into Parish Liturgies Is Vital

Virtually all the parishes profiled in this book incorporate bringing up the Sunday collection as an integral part of the offertory gifts.

Stewardship prayers and hymns with stewardship themes all help to carry stewardship into the realm of the sacred, where it indeed belongs. Preceding a Ministry Fair with a liturgical procession at Sunday Masses that feature banners of the various organizations and ministries is a striking way of calling attention to the time and talent dimension of stewardship (see Corpus Christi Parish, Chapter 1).

Inserting Stewardship Ideals into Classes of the RCIA (Rite of Christian Initiation of Adults)

Many churches find this a proactive move preparing the way for more generous giving and volunteering. Also productive are dinners for new members, at which the pastor can informally bring up what stewardship means in this parish, conveying expectations of proportional giving and of ministry involvement while increasing stewardship salience.

Envisioning Stewardship as an Invitation to Be "Prophetic"

Heeding the call to work with other civic and religious organizations addressing problems in the community can transform a parish, so virtually all the parishes studied in this book manifest this stewardship orientation, some outstandingly so, as we saw with the Basilica of Saint Mary in Chapter 7.

Stewardship Extends to Parishioners' Inner Lives

Prayerful consideration of one's gifts through the process of discernment, provision of growth in prayer, even reexamination leading to some retrenchment of parish "busy-ness" (see St. John the Baptist, Chapter 6) testify to the power of stewardship to evoke inner reflection as well as intense outgoing activity.

Truly, in a word, the promise of stewardship is *transformative*. All agree, it is a long-range strategy, years in the making. Yet I believe that by being holistic, stewardship has a basic advantage over other renewal strategies mentioned in the Introduction. Its core theology of *ourselves as gifted and asked to give back* encourages us to be responsibly generous disciples of Christ in sharing what has been bestowed on us, inducing a spirit of high intentionality within a parish. All facets of parish life, every aspect of ministry falls under scrutiny as stewardship takes hold. "Are we doing the best we can (in this area, this project, etc.)? Are we being faithful to the mission statement we have written? How can we do this better?" As one Stewardship Committee chair said to me, "Heck, if we're giving back our gifts to God, we want to make sure they're our *best* gifts."

I think that is exactly the idea. Father Michael O'Connell, rector of the Basilica of Saint Mary, alluded to Dietrich Bonhoeffer's warning against cheap grace in *The Cost of Discipleship:* "Anything that is worth anything *costs*. It costs time, energy, money. And nobody is selling anything more valuable than the Gospel of Jesus Christ."

Just so.

Appendix

Stewardship Interview Schedule

1. How did a stewardship approach begin in this parish? Did attendance at one or more NCSC or ICSC meetings play a role? Did the diocese (archdiocese) lend support to stewardship initiatives? Does the parish send delegates yearly to the National Catholic Stewardship Conference?

2. Has stewardship undergone new emphases or shifts since its inception? How would you describe these? How would you account for them?

3. Stewardship is often difficult to start up in a parish. Was that the case here? In what respects? If there were doubts and misgivings, how were these addressed?

4. Some parishes emphasize the "treasure" theme of stewardship during the fall pledge drive, saving the "time and talent" dimension for the spring. Is that the case here?

5. How are talents assessed? How are parishioners invited to give of their time and talents? What new ministry initiatives have arisen as a result of emphasis on giving of time and talent?

6. How are parishioners asked to give financially? Are parishioners encouraged to pledge? What proportion do so? Is working up to a full tithe (10 percent of gross income) held up as an ideal to strive for, or is some other form of proportionate giving emphasized? Are the various age groups in the parish approached differently and distinctively in this respect? How has giving increased since stewardship was introduced in the parish?

7. How is stewardship preached and how often, e.g., only during fall pledge drive/spring talent recruitment or more frequently? What themes have you found in talking about stewardship that resonate positively with parishioners? Do lay witnesses make presentations occasionally?

8. How is stewardship expressed in the liturgy, in music? Does it come into RCIA classes?

9. Are stewardship themes carried over into capital campaigns? How? Are collections taken for distinct drives, e.g., for missions, annual appeal, apart from regular giving? If so, is an effort made to relate them to stewardship?

10. It is sometimes said that stewardship obeys the "80-20 principle," i.e., that only a relatively small proportion of parishioners really internalize and practice it in their lives and that they "carry" the rest of the parish. Is that the case here?

11. Do you see stewardship as countercultural? If so, how?

12. Has stewardship in this parish carried over into setting up an endowment? Is there an effort to encourage parishioners to include the parish in their wills or in other forms of planned giving?

Bibliography

Archdiocese of St. Louis. *Strategic Pastoral Plan: 1999–2002.* St. Louis: The Catholic Center, 1999.

Baumann, John. *Fostering Discernment in a Parish Community.* Master of Divinity Thesis, School of Theology and Ministry, Seattle University, 1998.

Becker, Penny Edgell. *Congregations in Conflict: Cultural Models of Local Religious Life.* New York: Cambridge University Press, 1999.

Bonhoeffer, Dietrich. *The Cost of Discipleship.* New York: Macmillan, 1968.

Brennan, Patrick J. *Re-Imagining the Parish.* New York: Crossroad, 1990.

_____. *Parishes That Excel.* New York: Crossroad, 1992.

Campbell, Deanna. "A Lasting Legacy: Many Basilica Ministries Have Roots in the Care Guild." *Basilica* (Spring 1997) 17.

Champlin, Joseph M. *Sharing Treasure, Time and Talent: A Parish Manual for Sacrificial Giving or Tithing.* Collegeville, Minn.: The Liturgical Press, 1982.

D'Antonio, William V., James D. Davidson, Dean R. Hoge, and Katherine Meyer. *American Catholic Laity in a Changing Church.* Kansas City, Mo.: Sheed & Ward, 1989.

D'Antonio, William V. "Parish Catholics: It Makes a Difference." *National Catholic Reporter,* October 29, 1999.

Davidson, James D. "Increasing Indifference to Church Is Concern." *National Catholic Reporter,* October 29, 1999, 15.

Davidson, James D., and others [Andrea S. Williams, Richard A. Lamanna, Jan Stenftenagel, Kathleen Maas Weigert, William J. Whalen, and Patricia Wittberg, S.C.]. *The Search for Common Ground: What Unites and Divides Catholic Americans.* Huntington, Ind.: Our Sunday Visitor Press, 1997.

Deets, Chris. "Financial Stewardship: Greater Commitment Needed to Ease Budget Concerns." *Basilica* (Autumn 1996) 7.

Diocese of Oakland. *Faith in Service to the World: Recommendations for Action.* Oakland, Calif., 1994.

DiPiazza, Francesca. "Joe Sulentich: Coming Home to be Healed." *Basilica* (Winter 1998) 9.

Etzioni, Amitai. *A Comparative Analysis of Complex Organizations.* Glencoe, Ill.: Free Press, 1975.

Hoge, Dean R., and others [Michael J. Donahue, Patrick H. McNamara, and Charles E. Zech]. *Money Matters: Personal Giving in American Churches.* Louisville: John Knox/Westminster Press, 1996. See also Patrick McNamara and Charles Zech. "Lagging Stewards." *America* (September 14, 1996) 9–14.

Johnson, Mary, and others [Dean R. Hoge, William Dinges, and Juan L. Gonzales, Jr.]. "Young Adult Catholics: Conservative? Alienated? Suspicious?" *America* (March 27, 1999) 11.

McNamara, Patrick H. *More Than Money: Portraits of Transformative Stewardship.* Bethesda, Md.: The Alban Institute, 1999.

National Conference of Catholic Bishops. *Stewardship: A Disciple's Response: A Pastoral Letter on Stewardship.* Washington, D.C.: United States Catholic Conference, 1993.

_____. Ad Hoc Committee on Stewardship. *Stewardship and Development in Catholic Dioceses and Parishes: Resource Manual.* Washington, D.C.: United States Catholic Conference, 1996.

Putnam, Robert. *Bowling Alone: The Collapse and Revival of American Community.* New York: Simon and Schuster, 2000.

Schoenherr, Richard, and Lawrence Young. *Full Pews and Empty Altars.* Madison, Wis.: University of Wisconsin Press, 1993.

Shapiro, Ivan. *What God Allows: The Crisis of Faith and Conscience in One Catholic Church.* New York: Doubleday, 1996.

Sweetser, S.J., Thomas P. "The 'Good Enough' Pastor." *America* (September 25, 1999) 8–11.

_____. "Rx for Ailing Parishes: Change the Tone, Involve Everyone, Turn Outward." *Commonweal* (September 11, 1996) 20.

Sweetser, S.J., Thomas P., and Patricia M. Forster, O.S.F. *Transforming the Parish: Models for the Future.* Kansas City: Sheed and Ward, 1993.

Wuthnow, Robert. *The Crisis in the Churches: Spiritual Malaise, Fiscal Woe.* New York: Oxford University Press, 1997.

_____. *Poor Richard's Principle: Recovering the American Dream Through the Moral Dimension of Work, Business, and Money.* Princeton: Princeton University Press, 1996.

Zech, Charles E., and others [Patrick H. McNamara and Dean R. Hoge]. "Lagging Stewards—Part Two: Catholics as Church Volunteers." *America* (February 8, 1997) 22.

Zech, Charles E. *Why Catholics Don't Give . . . And What Can Be Done About It.* Huntington, Ind.: Our Sunday Visitor Press, 2000.